TEN THINGS YOUR TEEN WILL THANK YOU FOR... Someday

TEN THINGS YOUR TEEN WILL THANK YOU FOR...
Someday

William L. Coleman

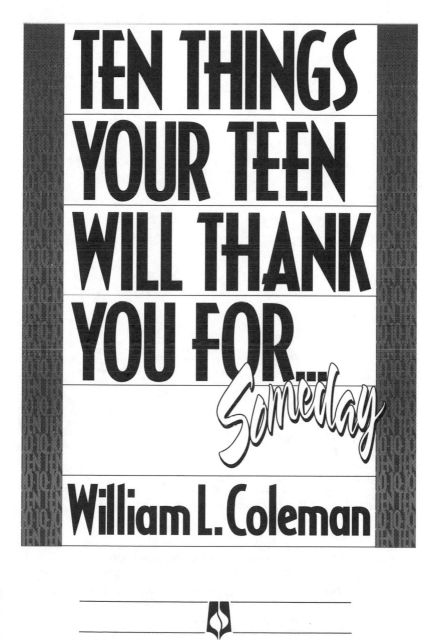

BETHANY HOUSE PUBLISHERS
MINNEAPOLIS, MINNESOTA 55438

Copyright © 1992
William L. Coleman
All Rights Reserved

Published by Bethany House Publishers
A Ministry of Bethany Fellowship, Inc.
6820 Auto Club Road, Minneapolis, Minnesota 55438

Printed in the United States of America

Library of Congress Cataloging-in-Publication Data

Coleman, William L.
　　Ten things your teen will thank you for/William L. Coleman
　　　　p.　　cm.
　　1. Parent and teenager—United States.
2. Parenting—Religious aspects—Christianity.　　I. Title.
HQ799.15.1C65　　　1992
649'.125—dc20　　　　　　　　　　　　　　　　91-46588
ISBN 1–55661–249–4　　　　　　　　　　　　　　　　CIP

Dedicated to the Big Three . . .

MARY, JIM, JUNE

for taking us through the school of life,

for being good teachers,

and being patient while we learned.

WILLIAM L. COLEMAN is the well-known author of over thirty Bethany House books on a variety of topics. Combining his experience as a pastor, researcher, writer, and speaker, he is noted for his effective communication in the area of family relationships and practical spirituality. He has been married for over twenty-five years and is the father of three children.

A Note From the Author

I Wish I'd Known Then . . .

When our children were born I wanted to be a perfect parent. Brought up in a truly dysfunctional family, I knew exactly what not to do. Deliberately, I began to devise a plan that would avoid all the pitfalls of my family of origin.

Naturally, I succeeded. I avoided the old mistakes, but in the process made new and creative mistakes of my own. The big factor I had not calculated was individuality—each teenager is his or her own person. Ultimately, they make the decisions about who they want to be.

Not that we failed. I am happy for our grown children and love each of them as they love us. But as I look back, I give the parental scream: "I wish I'd known then what I know now!"

Our family is like everyone else's family. We have been on the mountain-top as well as flat on our stomachs in the valley. I have been in the principal's office for all three of our teenagers. I was there because they had very high I.Q.'s. I was there because they won awards and honors. I was there because the administration wanted to throw them out. I was there when they were nominated for home-

7

coming royalty, and I was there when the police came at 3:00 A.M.

We are a real family. We want every reader to know that. If you're looking for wisdom gleaned from a we-have-it-all-together family, you picked up the wrong book. I suggest you try to get a refund. But if you want some idea of what really counts in raising teenagers, this book could be a big help.

The idea for this book first came to me when I asked a group at a seminar to write down what they thought their parents did right. The response was so warm that I began asking other groups and individuals. They welcomed the opportunity to reflect on the good memories of their childhood and adolescence.

My wife and I also heard from our own children. They told us what they considered valuable and what didn't really matter in their past. It was an eye-opener. We realized then how often we had majored in minors and minored in majors.

The entire experience of looking back on our parenting has been good. We are now able to thank God all over again for each member of our family.

We pray that this book will help parents of all ages: those who look forward to having teenagers, those who have them, and those who look back with great love and appreciation.

We want to thank Carol Johnson of Bethany House Publishers for her enthusiasm about the book. We also thank the many people who were willing to share.

> Bill and Pat Coleman
> Thanksgiving Eve

Contents

LETTERS
HOME

Children are master teachers. They are very aware
of what is going on, and they become even more
clearly aware as they grow through adolescence. As
teenagers they bewilder us, challenge us, satisfy us,
and sometimes even break our hearts. When we have
some idea of what is really lasting and important, we
are better able to supply the attitudes and events that
might last them a lifetime.

During a break at a seminar in Hordville, Nebraska, a friendly gentleman drew his wallet from his
pocket and asked me if I wanted to see something. I
figured it was pictures of his grandchildren and I was
already starting to form my "oohs" and "aahs." Instead, it was a piece of paper.

"This is a letter my girl sent me. She's in college
now." His face beamed like every proud father's
should.

I unfolded the letter to find one page of total praise
and gratitude for her terrific dad. There were no if's
or but's; no hidden messages or complaints. The page
was a chorus of appreciation for the many things he

had done and for the person he was.

In this one letter a daughter had set her father free from any doubts and made him feel like a fulfilled person. He no longer had to worry about the things he hadn't done. She told him he had done it right.

Not everyone is going to get a letter like that. Many parents will get a warm hug and a general thank-you-for-everything. That means a great deal in itself. Unfortunately, some very good parents will never hear and can only guess how well they may have done.

When grown children do communicate—and it isn't always easy for them—they give us a clear idea of what was important during their formative years. Often they thank their parents for unusual things. Most often they are personal experiences; seldom are they expensive. Many young adults are embarrassed that their parents spent so much money on them. They seem far more grateful for the examples of Christian faith, and less impressed with the lectures.

Some parents have received the same information by simply asking their children. One father I know sat at the dining room table and asked open-ended, non-threatening questions. What kind of discipline do you think was the most effective? What was your favorite vacation? What were some good Christmas memories?

Not pulling for compliments, we can give the opportunity and listen to what makes their eyes sparkle. All parents should have the pleasure of knowing how often they did meaningful and important things for their teenagers.

A Letter From June

A couple of years ago I received one of those magical letters. At that time our twenty-two-year-old daughter was in St. Louis for the summer working with inner-city children.

The letter I received from June that summer was filled with appreciation for her dad, and broke my heart with joy. I have asked June for permission to publish the letter because I believe it explains the purpose of this book.

Parts of the letter will seem vague, but I didn't want to edit it in any way. It's real and it's spontaneous. The only exception is that I changed the name of the cousin. Our attempts to evade the cousin were in fun and I'm sure every family can understand those maneuverings.

Dear Daddy,

I remember how exciting it was to hop into the front seat of my Daddy's flower truck. I remember when I gave him a stick of Big Red gum, and he didn't even get mad when it stuck to his dentures. He knew it would, but he wanted to accept my gift. I remember piling into the big old Buick, just my Dad and me, and going to Nebraska football games. I remember the infamous strawberry pie at Big Boy Shoney's. I remember playing *move up* in Streeters Park. I remember my Dad trying to cut my jeans out of my bicycle chain after they got caught and ending up running home naked, my jeans still with the bike. I remember beaming as my Dad starred in community theater productions. I remember being gently baptized in the river. I remember the fragrance of Daddy fanning his arms in front of the car air conditioner. It meant so much to be able to take family vacations; hiking in Estes Park, blowing the radiator in North Carolina, together trying to dodge cousin Arnold at the family reunion. I owe my love of the city to him. I can remember watching *Roots* and asking him if I could marry a black person. He said only to make sure he was the best man in the world for his little girl. That incident alone helped to shape many of my feelings and attitudes for equality. I remember sponsoring a Laotian family and what an example that set for me. I remember Daddy pulling the seams of the family together when everything seemed to be pulling them apart.

I remember killing the engine 30 times in the new stick-shift while he patiently said, "Almost. Try again . . ." I remember proudly showing all the third-graders my Daddy's first book during show-and-tell. I remember the excitement of every Saturday night in Salisbury because I could call home. I jump out of bed for late-night phone calls because I know it's my Dad. He always finds the right thing to say.

I remember his complacency each time I wrecked his car. "Aren't you mad YET?!" I cherish midnight donut runs, mid-morning coffee. I miss these things.

He is exceptionally level-headed, undeniably compassionate. He never has to win anything. He tries harder than any parent's expected to. He is quick to forgive, slow to anger—the epitome of the love contained in First Corinthians.

He has taught me to cry when I needed to, but stop when I should. He has taught me to fight for justice, to live to serve. I've learned to *chill* when life became too serious. He's understood and listened (and cried) when I needed to sever relationships. From him, I learned to be courageously independent, to take risks.

My Father has shown me a peace worth discovering and I'm still working at it.

I love you, Daddy!

June

Letting Me Dream, Even If Some of Them Were Nightmares

One hundred fifty years ago a new word was coined: larky. A larky is someone who chases larks. Larks are illusive singing birds and people chase them playfully, simply for the fun of it.

If we are fortunate, we have children who are larkys. They grow up chasing dreams. Larkys are not looneys. Larkys are sane people who stretch their imagination and take risks. They hunger to try new things, go new places, and experience all the possibilities.

The parents of larkys are called chauffeurs. In the early years they spend a great deal of time driving their children to ball games, to contests, to parks, to campaign rallies, to schools, to cities. Their larkys want to see, hear, feel, learn, and try for themselves.

When they become teenagers they can do the driving, but until then larkys need chauffeurs.

Never call the chauffeurs of a larky backstage parents. They don't need to push their children into every event under the sun. Larky children begin running at their own pace and dare their parents to try and keep up with them.

What a larky needs most from parents is the answer to this question: Is it all right to dream? A parent can reply no and throw cold water on this creative youth. That won't necessarily stop him or her, but it will prove an obstacle.

On the other hand, parents can give clear, positive signals and encourage their young person by freeing him or her to explore. We can give the message by words, by modeling, and by attitude. Children who are permitted the luxury of dreaming have a warm place in their hearts for understanding parents.

Finding Her Own Path

When our daughter, June, was barely sixteen, she already had a long history of dream-chasing. A joiner, she never met an organization she didn't want to be part of and never joined a group she didn't want to be president of within two weeks. As every parent knows, age sixteen means that June now had a driver's license and wanted to borrow the car. (Most parents want the driving age raised to 35, to avoid the high insurance premiums.)

Barely familiar with driving, June soon announced her dream. She had met a great guy who lived a hundred miles away in Podunk, Nebraska. To get there she would have to drive around the city of Lincoln by way of Interstate 80 and then cover 25 miles of back-country roads.

June had planned a daytime date and would return home before dark. She had thought it all through and simply wanted the car and a hearty farewell.

The boy had been to our home and we felt good about him. The question was how did we feel about June? The long trip away, driving by herself, was a scary thought. In the case of a son, parents figure being stranded on a highway somewhere will probably do him some good. But the prospect of your unprotected little girl with a stalled car is soul-wrenching.

We tried to negotiate. What if I drove her? Out of the question. What if I just drove her to Lincoln and waited in a mall for her return? Totally unnecessary, she insisted.

Finally we agreed to let June chase her dream. Crestfallen, I handed her the keys at the appointed time. Half-convinced I would never see June again, I bade her happy motoring. She backed out of the driveway (without looking) and drove off into the wicked world by herself.

Any parent knows how traumatic that was for us. Dream-letting isn't easy. It comes close to bloodletting. But remember how we felt when our parents rained on our parades? We wanted to find out for ourselves. We wanted to make our own mistakes. We gladly traded security for freedom. We wanted protection, but we also wanted permission to follow rainbows.

Casting Your Bread Upon the Waters

Creative children may emerge from dull homes, but only with great difficulty. Surrounded by a shut-down mentality, they must struggle to free themselves from an atmosphere of caution and hesitancy. But young people who know that dreaming is al-

lowed at home are far more likely to have visions—
in vivid color.

The author of Ecclesiastes entices the reader with
the invitation to take chances: "Cast your bread upon
the waters, for after many days you will find it again"
(11:1).

A spirit of adventure lives in some families. Physical, spiritual, mental adventures dare everyone to try
something new. Not reckless adventure that dares
everyone to get hurt, but creative challenges that encourage everyone to at least try.

The same spirit is found in Proverbs 11:24: "One
man gives freely, yet gains even more; another withholds unduly, but comes to poverty."

Nothing ventured, nothing gained. Young people
catch the spirit of adventure from their parents, when
they see them give freely, cast their bread upon the
waters, and make their own dreams come true.

When a young person sees his or her parents take
chances, that young person is far more likely to do
the same. For example, parents who go out as short-
term missionaries, who conduct home Bible studies,
who feed the hungry in their own city, and who sacrifice their time and talents for others, give their teenagers the example of adventure. They are risk-takers.
By taking certain risks, they give their young people
unspoken permission to dream and to get involved
in their own concrete adventures.

Our friend Cliff cast his bread upon the waters by
getting involved in digging wells in Haiti. His will-
ingness to go year after year, to give, to tell others,
has resulted in scores of other people traveling there
and working.

Cliff took the risk, not knowing what to expect, or
what would happen. The good results have been multiplied over and over.

Teenagers should be exposed to more than temporary dreams. Don't limit them to visions of bigger houses and faster cars. There are spiritual dreams they need to be challenged with. Sharing Christ, giving hope to the hopeless, counseling friends, praying for people in need, and working soup kitchens are spiritual dreams. Touching the souls and hearts of others are dreams that we all can make come true.

Not that parents should receive all the credit. Teenagers eventually must decide to be adventurous on their own. But we can furnish a few springboards.

Ice-crushers

Some parents pride themselves on their ability to crush dreams. Under too much heat dreams melt away. Under too much pressure they break into pieces. Ice-crushers believe their contribution is to see what is wrong with a dream and try to smash it.

Although the intent may have been to simply spare the child by destroying the dream, ice-crushers also tend to destroy the dreamer.

If a parent is negative and overly cautious, the child tends to react in one of two ways: Either the child tries not to dream because he or she senses that dreaming could be dangerous, or the child continues to dream but withholds those dreams from the ice-crusher—the parent.

Proverbs tells us how painful a crushed spirit is: "A cheerful heart is good medicine, but a crushed spirit dries up the bones" (17:22).

All of us have suffered at one time or other from a crushed spirit, perhaps many times. But the most severe kind of broken spirit comes from our parents. When a parent says our ideas are dumb, we assume they know us better than anyone else. It's hard for a child's spirit to rise up after parental disapproval.

That bit of obvious knowledge won't stop the dedicated ice-crusher. They are convinced of the value of bubble-bursting. They think every issue should be totally scrutinized. They want each negative eliminated before anything goes forward.

Young people love to hear the words, "Why not give it a shot?"

Sitting and Biting

The parents who bless dreams know when to sit on their hands and bite their tongues. It starts early—when Monte tries to hook up the television set to the electric garage door opener. He figures Dad can turn on the news as he parks the car.

Mom walks out of the kitchen, and Sarah decides to add mushrooms to the chocolate chip cookies. She thinks it will give them a pizza flavor.

I think God does the same for us. He must be tempted to intervene, to protect us, to keep us safe. But our Heavenly Father lets us go, to chase our dreams while He sits on His hands and bites His tongue, so to speak. God doesn't take our choices away. He knows we could mess up, but He lets us have that opportunity.

Conservative homes are usually big on holding back. Risk-taking is not one of their main features. Conservative families don't like to experiment and load up on novel ideas. They like to be careful, cautious, and keep their cool. If that's the case, they shouldn't be terribly surprised if their children are reluctant to wonder and dream.

Risk-takers are the children who dabble with new ideas. They dare to imagine things they have not yet seen. In its purest form it is faith in the true biblical concept: "Now faith is being sure of what we hope for and certain of what we do not see" (Heb. 11:1).

How do non-dreaming families produce children

who dream? They let go and encourage their children to go for it. It happens all the time. Parents who didn't go out for the school play when they were teenagers allow and encourage their own children to take that chance. Parents who never traveled when they were young permit their young people to go to Costa Rica as summer missionaries. If we couldn't let go and chase our dreams, we can still allow our young people to cut loose and rattle after theirs.

I think every parent should have one child who enjoys the piano, one artist of the ivories who practices gladly without parental nagging. June was our gift to the metronome.

She learned to play early and quickly. Gifted with perfect pitch, June was loaded with talent and the joy of playing the piano. As she approached college, she naturally applied for a music scholarship. However, she insisted on applying for a *voice* scholarship, not piano.

Now, June has an excellent voice, but we all thought her greater gift was in piano. Yet who were we to tell her what dreams to chase? What do mere parents, teachers and musicians know? My wife and I sat on our hands and bit our tongues.

Eventually the word came. Our daughter had received her scholarship to the university, in voice. She felt great and we breathed a collective sigh of relief. June had made her dream come true. But because she'd never had a voice lesson, the going was *extremely* rough. A voice instructor said to her that first year, "If you've never had a voice lesson, why are you here?"

Year after year she fought the battles, always struggling uphill. Today she is a senior honor roll student who did it her way.

Were we wrong? Should we have tried harder to steer her toward a piano major? Without anyone's interference June followed the rainbow and found her own pot of gold.

Instead of making decisions for our children, one of the best things we can do is broaden their outlook. If they want to go into business we might get some literature on business-related subjects. That's gentle guidance. We might offer to take them places and help them meet people who are knowledgeable in the field.

If a young person is great at math, his or her parents might think their child should pursue something in that field. But simply because the young person is good at something doesn't mean he or she would enjoy it as a career. Teenagers who are allowed to pursue their dreams—rather than chase after their parents' dream—are far more likely to strive with the energy and stamina it will take to achieve that goal.

Continually we meet adults whose parents crushed their spirits, burst their bubbles, rained on their parades. They resented the interference, and some still carry that resentment.

Thanks for the Nightmares

We are all entitled to a few good nightmares. Each of us should have the experience of waking up in the middle of the night in a cold sweat. We should be allowed to say to ourselves, "I really messed up this time. What in the world am I going to do?"

If we encourage children to admit their mistakes, we set them free to handle life openly and honestly. Openly admitting their error allows them to try new adventures, knowing that it's all right to either succeed or fail. Messing up isn't life's greatest tragedy. Being afraid to try new things is a far worse misfortune.

Permission to create nightmares will help instill

honesty in our youth. How many people do we know who lie about their mistakes? These people mess up and then work hard trying to cover up. Afraid to admit failure, they waste much energy and creativity trying to deny their mistakes.

Every young person should know that it's normal to mess up and it's healthy to admit it. Teenagers may one day thank their parents for letting them have their own nightmares. Nightmares are part of the dream process.

POWER
FOR LIVING®

NOVEMBER 8, 1992

"MAYBE JESUS WILL HELP HIM"

These words echoed in Geoff Case's ears as he sought to find a victim of drowning in a murky Thai river. Turn to page 2 to learn what happened.

ALL IN A DAY'S WORK TO RAISE THE DEAD

The Lord sometimes performs miracles to confirm the Gospel. But would He today?

**BY GEOFF CASE as told to
DEBRA FLEETWOOD WOOD**

Editor: ROY IRVING • *Managing Editor:* DON CRAWFORD • *Editorial Assistant:* MABEL HOWARD
Design: DAVID FRYKHOLM • *Production:* STEPHEN HANCY

POWER FOR LIVING, a POWER/Line paper for adults, is published quarterly in weekly parts by SP PUBLICATIONS, INC. Yearly subscriptions available. Subscription addresses: SP PUBLICATIONS, Box 632, Glen Ellyn, IL 60138; SP PUBLICATIONS, LTD., Box 2000, Paris, ON N3L 3X5, Canada; SP FOUNDATION (U.K.) LTD., Raans Road, Amersham-on-the-Hill, Bucks. HP6 6JQ, England. © 1992, SP PUBLICATIONS, INC. All rights reserved. Scripture quotations marked "NIV" are from the *Holy Bible, New International Version,* © 1973, 1978, 1984, International Bible Society, used by permission of Zondervan Bible Publishers. Unless otherwise indicated, copyright of by-lined articles is owned exclusively by the authors. No part of this paper may be reproduced in any form without written permission. Printed in U.S.A.

Vol. 50, No. 4 Sept • Oct • Nov 1992

The weathered Thai barges bobbed up and down heedlessly while the people at the river's edge thronged and milled like stockyard sheep. One woman screamed and sobbed convulsively and the man near her wept. But his eyes occasionally raised to watch the men treading water in the brown river.

I sat at a coffee shop table watching my Thai students discuss their Christian faith with some local Buddhist gentlemen. But the riverside crowd kept pulling my eyes from their debate. I wondered what drama was causing such a commotion.

We had come from the Bible an hour earlier, their child had fallen overboard, and by now had drowned. "No one has been able to find the body, and you know what that means." He shook his head.

Yes, I knew. Thais believe that as soon as someone dies, the disembodied spirit enters a state of limbo. Unless the family cremates the body within one week, the tormented spirit will come to terrorize them. What an extra sadness, to be afraid of your own beloved child!

It also meant that if one of the swimmers managed to locate and retrieve the child's body, they could ask any price — even a month's wages — and the poor parents would

"*Jesus really did help him!*" the crowd repeated to each other

school where I taught at Phayao, Thailand, to Hunka township for a practical evangelism training week. We had prepared skits, Bible messages, and brought films to project from the back of our Land Rover.

The novelty had drawn around 200 each night, but as the projector flickered off, the crowd melted into the black night and we packed our things alone. No one accepted our invitation to stay and receive Christ.

The few local Christians in Hunka provided contacts for daytime calls. After a morning of this, we were enjoying Cokes and conversation at the local coffee shop. But I couldn't keep my eyes from wandering to the people across the river. I summoned the waiter.

"What is happening?" I asked in careful Thai.

He explained that the weeping couple were salesmen who had boated up from Bangkok. About half

be obliged to pay.

I thought of my own wonderful young sons, Andy and Paul. How would I feel if I were in these people's positions? This family had no hope of heaven, no comfort from the Lord. I couldn't imagine the blackness of their grief. But I could easily see its manifestations in their hysteria. They needed the Lord.

But what could I do? I often taught my students that the Lord sometimes performs signs and wonders to confirm the Gospel preaching. He did it when Paul and Silas preached in a town (Acts 4), just as we were doing in this one. But would He today?

Leaving my friends, I walked toward the mourners. "May I borrow your sarong?" I asked the tallest bystander I could find. I carefully secured his skimpy linen aroud my

Continued on page 7

I HATED AUNT GUSTY

BY LEON JONES

I didn't know my words would become a stinging indictment against myself

I hate you!" I heard my daughter's angry voice from inside the house.

"I didn't *mean* to lose your Frisbee!" came her brother's frustrated response.

On the back porch, my wife Joye and I ignored the conflict. Like most brothers and sisters, 16-year-old Doug and 13-year-old Laura argued from time to time.

We could hear Laura stalking across the den floor toward the back door. Swinging it open, she exclaimed, "Daddy, Doug threw my Frisbee into the sewer!"

By this time Doug was outside, pleading his cause. "It was an accident!"

"But why did you sneak into my room and steal my Frisbee?" Laura demanded.

"Did you take it from her room, Son?" I asked.

He lowered his head. "Well — yeah."

"I believe you owe your sister an apology," I said sternly.

"I *tried* to apologize, Dad," Doug said. "I even told her I'd pay for the Frisbee. But she won't listen to me."

I wrapped an arm around Laura's shoulder. "The Bible teaches us to forgive," I reminded.

"I know, but I'm still mad at him!" Her refusal to forgive surprised me. Most of the time, Laura exhibits her mother's easy-going disposition. I was sure she would soon get over the incident.

But three days later Laura was still upset with Doug. I decided a discussion about Christ expecting us to forgive was in order. I didn't know that my words would soon become a stinging indictment against myself.

As I was lecturing Laura, the phone rang. It was my cousin Clarence, reminding me about our family reunion the coming weekend. "We can count on you and your family being there, can't we?"

I assured him that he could, then I asked, "Who all will be there?"

"The same group as always," Clarence replied, "and Aunt Gusty is coming down from Tennessee."

Oh, no! I thought. *She's the last person I want to see.*

I had never liked Aunt Gusty. She'd lived with my family off and on when I was a boy. For some reason, she seemed to receive pleasure in making me feel that I was considerably less that I should be. "The Lord must have run out of brains

when He got to you," she often told me. She frequently compared me unfavorably with my older brother, the star pitcher on our high school baseball team and an A student.

"Are you still there?" Clarence asked, interrupting my reverie.

"Uh—yes."

"OK, then we'll see you at—"

"Clarence!" I blurted out, wondering how I could tell him that I did *not* want to see Aunt Gusty. "I just remembered: I've got something I have to do this weekend—a business seminar. I'm sorry, but we won't be able to make it to the reunion this year." Then I hung up.

I turned around to see Joye and the children staring at me, puzzled looks on their faces. The children and their mother had been looking forward to the reunion. It had always been the highlight of our year.

Joye asked why we weren't going.

I told her I'd forgotten about the "business seminar."

Doug said that my mother had called yesterday and said that she was looking forward to the reunion.

I stuttered an explanation that I must have forgotten to tell Mother about the seminar.

Guilt followed me the rest of the week. I became depressed for deceiving my family, and for hating Aunt Gusty.

At supper Friday night Joye sat gazing thoughtfully at me. I had never been able to keep anything from her very long. After the meal, I took her aside and told her the truth: I did not want to go to the reunion if Aunt Gusty would be there.

Joye finally convinced me that I really needed to confront the person who had caused me to carry such anger. It had been buried deep inside for too long.

So the next morning we picked Mother up and headed for the North Georgia mountains. That afternoon we drove to the country church where the family reunion was to be held. Mother climbed out of the car and embraced her older sister. *Thank God, it's not Aunt Gusty,* I told myself.

It had been years since I had last seen her, but I was certain that I would be able to recognize Aunt Gusty. She had always been a short stout woman with thin lips that rarely relaxed into anything resembling a smile.

My mother's oldest brother usually asked the blessing for the food. But today he announced, "I'd like to ask my sister Gusty to return thanks for our food today."

A thin woman with bony arms and chalk-white face rose slowly from her seat directly across from me. I never would have guessed her to be Aunt Gusty! I later learned that she had been diagnosed as having cancer of the liver, and had only a few more months to live—which was why she had decided to attend this family reunion.

As Aunt Gusty prayed, I kept my eyes on her, amazed at the sharp contrast of what I had expected her to look like and how she actually looked. She spoke in a raspy voice that revealed the pain she was experiencing.

After the meal, the older people sat around talking about their childhood while Cousin Clarence organized a volleyball game. We played for an hour, then joined the family for a hymn sing in the church.

We were bellowing out "Standing on the Promises" when Aunt Gusty came over and stood next to me. Leaning down, she whispered, "Could I have a word with you?"

I pretended not to hear.

"Please talk to me, Leon."

I looked up into her wrinkled face, but continued singing. She did not move.

"OK," I said with resignation. I got up and followed her outside the church. We stood on the front steps. I didn't trust myself to speak, so I said nothing.

Aunt Gusty finally broke the silence. "I've thought about you a lot lately."

I didn't know what to say. "How have you been?" I managed.

"Tolerably well." After a pause, she continued. "I know you must hate me, and I don't blame you if you do. But I'm an old woman now, and I don't have much longer to live."

She looked deep into my eyes. "Please forgive me," she said, wiping the heels of her hands at the tears springing from her eyes.

I glanced back inside the church at my family. Doug and Laura sat together, their confrontation over the Frisbee forgotten now. My lecture to Laura about forgiveness came ringing into my ears.

Turning back to Aunt Gusty, I said, "All I ever wanted was for you to love me."

"I did, Leon. I just didn't know how to show it." She reached out for my hand. I didn't resist as she cupped it in her bony fingers. "I was saved a few months ago. I know God forgives me. Now I need you to forgive me. Please."

"I—" Tears erupted from my eyes. I stabbed at them with my fingers, but they rolled over my hand and down my face. "I forgive you, Aunt Gusty."

As the words crossed my lips, a warm sensation washed over me, cleansing me of the bitterness I had felt for this woman. Holding her hand, I led her back inside the church.

Aunt Gusty requested that we sing her favorite hymn, and soon the old church was rocking to the joyful sound of "Will the Circle Be Unbroken?"

After the last hymn was sung, families said their good-byes and slowly began piling into cars. Our station wagon was soon chugging up a steep mountain road.

Mother took her Bible from her purse and read aloud about Christ's promise to His believers about a glorious reunion in heaven one day. "Pick a hymn, Leon," Mother said.

I thought about Aunt Gusty, and about my new love for her. I marveled at the Lord's grace and the power of forgiveness. "How about 'Will the Circle Be Unbroken?' "

We sang it all the way home. □

waist and hoped it wouldn't slide off as I wriggled out of my clothes underneath.

Wading into the filthy current, I prayed silently. *Lord, help me find this child's body for the sake of Your glory and Your Gospel.* But down deep I had little faith that I could find it. The current, running swiftly through this portion of the river below the dam, could have pushed it miles downstream.

I had done a bit of skin diving back home in Australia. But any underwater search skills I had learned in the crystal-blue Pacific would be useless in this soup.

The last thing I heard as I ducked under was the onlookers whispering to each other "Maybe Jesus will help him. Maybe Jesus will help him." I hoped against hope that they were right.

In order to get my bearings, I first dived to the bottom of the river. It was deeper than I had expected, and as opaque as gravy. *This is not going to be easy,* I thought to myself. On my second descent, I swam straight into a soft form wedged in a tree trunk.

I wrestled the body free of the entangling limbs and kicked upwards. When my head erupted from the surface, I gulped air hungrily. Instantly a giant gasp rose from the crowd. "Jesus really did help him!" They repeated the words to each other incredulously.

I towed the body to shore and placed it before the waiting parents. The father knelt down next to his son's body and began slapping him, then kissing him. "Wake up! Wake up!" he repeated louder and louder. He flung himself on top of the body and hugged it as if he could press life into the cold form.

I looked at the boy's face. He must have been around 16. Apparently, the boat's propeller had sliced into his skull. He had no doubt died instantly.

Finally, the parents rose to thank me and to see what I might charge. I politely declined their payment, bid them good-bye, and left to dress and rejoin my friends.

Amazed and elated that the Lord had answered my faltering prayer so quickly, I kept muttering, *Thank You, Jesus, Thank You, Jesus,* under my breath. But I felt the weight of sadness too, not only for the bereaved parents, but for people whose superstitions condemn them to grieve hopelessly.

These people were in bondage to Satan's deceit and only the Son of God Himself could set them free. I ached with longing that they and the other villagers would come to accept the gift of eternal life in Christ.

The whole event had taken only a few minutes, but it marked a milestone in my trust in the Lord. He had assured that His name would be gossiped all around this little town and perhaps some would be intrigued enough to want to hear more.

That night a much larger crowd turned out at the plaza to watch the film and hear the students preach. I prayed for the grieving family especially. I do not know if they came or were still too absorbed in their sudden loss. But I was sure they would always remember that it was Jesus who had the power to find their son.

Perhaps someday in heaven I will have the joy to recognize them or others who were witnesses of God's grace one humid afternoon in a muck-filled river. □

WHAT IS IN YOUR BACKPACK?

At home, it was hard to decide which items I really needed for a 50-mile backpacking trip in the White Mountains of New Hampshire. I wanted to be adequately prepared for all contingencies, so most of the questionable items went in the pack. With food and water, it weighed about 70 pounds.

At the end of the first day, after struggling over steep, rocky Mt. Moosilauke, I knew exactly what I didn't need. What the comfort of my living room couldn't reveal, the trail had made clear. I learned a lesson: Adversity redefines necessity.

I had two flashlights, two shirts and two pairs of trousers. My first aid kit could have supported an appendectomy. The list went on. All were things I thought I couldn't do without. Having to carry them over a mountain changed my mind.

I have looked back on that trip with a new understanding of the phrase, "walking with God." The life of faith is a footpath, not a freeway. Each traveler carries his own freight. There is no baggage service and no free ride. The first rule of the long-distance hiker should be mine as a Christian: Travel lightly.

Every day I walk with a spiritual backpack filled with things that masquerade as "necessities." Anger, pride, selfishness, and worry are foremost among them. They promise emotional freedom, but only serve to make the present more difficult. I can't stay on the trail and enjoy the scenery under all their weight. A heavy pack and a hurried pace set the stage for serious injury on the trail.

Paul told the Colossians: "You must rid yourselves of all such things as these: anger, rage, malice, slander, and filthy language from your lips" (Col. 3:8, NIV).

Unload them. Cast them away. Lay down the burdens of animosity and bitterness. Forgive as Christ has forgiven you.

Is there something in your backpack that needs to go? The word from experienced hikers is "Slow down, lighten up, savor the journey." □

Watching
Roots and
Meeting
Laotians

When I was a child living in Washington, D.C., an Afro-American family moved in across the street from us. The event was exciting for me. Although there were black families just a few blocks away, I didn't personally know anyone from another race.

I actually looked at it as a cross-cultural event. With the typical curiosity of a young child, I thought it would be neat to find out how another person lived and felt.

The family had a boy my age. He and I weren't allowed to attend the same school, even though we lived in the same neighborhood. I don't know where he went to school. That was a blank my young mind couldn't fill in.

It took us only a few minutes to become friends. We played together, though I don't remember exactly what we did. We even discussed racial epithets. I asked if he had ever been called the "ugly" word. He hadn't. In return he wanted to know if I had ever been called a "white cracker." I laughed. I had heard the term but no one had applied it to me directly.

There on the streets, a mere seven blocks from the nation's capitol, two children were hammering out the intricate details of racial relations. I liked my new friend and suspected he liked me, too. Immediately after school I looked for him excitedly, and we played together without a hitch.

We had only known each other for a matter of days when my mother confronted me. She wanted to know if I was playing with the black boy across the street. Enthusiastically I told her I was. She then shocked me by saying I was never to play with him again.

I must have been very young because I obeyed her immediately. But I also had no idea of the reason I had been forbidden the joy of playing with this new friend.

Soon the black family moved away. But the memory of my friend has never dimmed. Other friends have come and gone through the years, but this was a friendship literally stolen from me.

I have often wondered why adults didn't leave us alone. He and I could have worked it all out. We were off to a great start. We had no history of frustration, bigotry, emotional baggage or false pride. We simply accepted each other.

Parents Hold the Big Key

The keys to either kindling or quelling prejudice are found in many places. Schools, churches, relatives and friends each hold a key to the complicated set of locks that we call bigotry. There is no simple solution. But on that chain of keys there is one bigger than all the others. It is the parental key. We use it to lock or unlock the doors that form our children's outlook on people who are different from them.

Every child who has a Christian parent has a golden opportunity to resist prejudice. Although we are far from perfect, we have the ability to love one another as equals and to rise above the hate of bigotry, and instill that same behavior in our children by our example.

The debate is not whether we should march for equality or write our congressional representative. Our primary Christian function and responsibility is to share our love for all groups and to share that love in our own homes. We, who send missionaries to every race and nationality, play the hypocrite if we then denounce others in our own dining rooms.

The primary hope we have to seriously reduce prejudice is by freeing our children to explore a world full of contrasts. Parents must swallow their preconditioned emotions and give their children the permission to love others who are not the same as them. If there is little hope for stubborn adults, let there be promise for the children.

Too long Christians have said, "We are not into social issues." Meanwhile, we have spoken out against gambling and abortion while we defend war and capital punishment. Surely we can stretch ourselves enough to relieve our children of the burden of prejudice.

Give Permission

Parents aren't expected to force their children to love other people. The best gift may simply be to give them permission. "It's okay to love people who are different from us" is a message that opens a kaleidoscope of multicolored and shifting possibilities, which will serve our children well.

When we give permission, we are likely to see Hispanics, Native Americans, Afro-Americans, Asians, and Africans brought home by our children. Not only people visiting from mission stations, but also local friends whom they have met and feel free to introduce to their family.

These children aren't given an order to go out and drag in a minority. Rather, they receive approval to become friends with whomever they choose.

When the television series *Roots* was on, we watched much of it as a family. It wasn't a planned activity, but all of us seemed to flop in front of the tube at the same time. In the middle of one of the episodes, June, in grade school, popped this question from some place in left field:

"How would you feel, Dad, if I married a black guy?"

I spontaneously replied by saying what all dads are supposed to say to their young daughters: "Okay, as long as he's the greatest guy in the world for my girl."

Years later as a college student, June went to St. Louis to spend the summer working with inner-city children. In her letter home, June thanked me for what I had said while we watched *Roots.* She said it freed her up to accept black people as equals. Her father didn't swallow his coffee cup or go into a social dissertation. He didn't tell her she couldn't relate with people like that.

How parents treat others has a profound effect on children. Kids shouldn't have to spend their lives reacting to their parents' prejudices. They will work hard trying to agree with their parents' bigotry or they will work hard attempting to rebel against it. Be an example, but don't muddle up the process with heavy do's and don'ts. The most important gift you can give your children is the freedom to feel for themselves.

Peter found it difficult to accept Gentiles as equal (Acts 10). The last thing he wanted to do was take the Gospel to Cornelius at Caesarea. But, after some difficult lessons, Peter learned that God loves all people without favoritism (v. 34). Surely we can hand that simple truth down to our children without sending them through Peter's turmoil.

Hopefully our oldest daughter, Mary, felt she too had this magical "permission" when she spent that hot summer working with inner-city kids in Dallas. Or when she worked with troubled girls. Or now, when she works part-time at the public defender's office.

There are few things that parents can make their children feel. Compassion must be owned by the individual, on his terms, within his own heart. Grown children must wrestle with God over what pulls at their souls. Parents open the doors and set them free to pursue their sense of equality.

Examples Help

Words are empty without a context. If a mother or father says "love, love, love," but their actions say "hate, hate, hate," their children pick it up right away. Young people understand the difference between walk and talk, and it is the behavior, not the words, they are most likely to remember.

Children will recall seeing their parents working in soup kitchens, teaching at city missions, going to mission fields, giving clothes and furniture away. Those visual aids are imprinted on young minds and are seldom erased by age.

Frequently parents believe they provide terrible examples for their children. But no one asked us to be *perfect* examples. As children climb through the early grades, they soon learn that their parents have blemishes. Children can deal with that knowledge.

Despite our imperfect image, children still need the glimpses of Christlikeness in us. Even those brief pictures of us as examples of God's love and mercy are enough to inspire and stimulate our children.

No school system or church will teach as well as parents. Rock-bottom values are learned at the supper table, playing games in the family room, and camping on vacation. Parents get the first and best crack at instilling lasting qualities. Instead of worrying so much over what other influences might reach our children, we should first be concerned about the influence we have on them.

The Old Testament scenario still applies today: "Impress [God's commandments] on your children. Talk about them when you sit at home and when you walk along the road, when you lie down and when you get up" (Deut. 6:7).

The Laotians Are Coming

Like most families, we haven't had many earth-shaking events. Most of the time our lives consisted of buying shoes, mowing the lawn, and visiting state parks. But a few events have left lasting impressions on everyone in our family.

Ten years ago we were watching television and saw pictures of Laotian families penned in large detention camps. Pat and I felt urged by God to become involved in one family's situation. Soon we met with friends and a group was formed to bring a Laotian family to our little town of Aurora, Nebraska.

We told our children of the plan and invited them to jump in at any point where they felt like helping. Our goal was to serve Jesus Christ by helping this family, and those were the terms we used. We even put a jar on the table where anyone could give to assist in the finances we needed to pull this off.

The day came when we piled into cars and drove to Grand Island to pick up the Bouatick family. There we met Tou and Kim, their two daughters, Le and Loli and KhamPheo, a teenage girl related to them. All of their belongings only made up a few bundles.

We became fast friends even though the language barrier was nearly impossible. Each of us pointed, grunted and chuckled more than we actually spoke. One day Pat and Kim rolled on the floor in hysterical laughter, each of them fully aware that they had no idea what the other had been saying.

Our children tried to teach their children English and befriend them in school. Mary took a study hall especially designed to teach the English language to KhamPheo.

Their needs varied and we felt excited to be part of their lives. One time we announced to our family that we would be collecting clothes for the Bouatick family. If anyone had anything to send along, they could deposit it by the front door.

Before long Mary brought in two grocery bags and placed them on the floor. Her curious four-years-younger sister wandered over to the bags and started to rummage through the clothes Mary had donated.

"Mary," June protested. "These jeans are practically new."

"I know," Mary agreed, "but I have other jeans and KhamPheo doesn't have any."

You can't send your children to classes to learn attitudes like that. The best you can do is model and supply the opportunity. Usually it's contagious. More often they grow up to exceed anything you were ever involved in. Rigid moral lessons can't compare with the value of practical examples.

It's pretty hard to hate an entire race of people when you have met a few who are terrific. It's difficult to believe stereotypes when you have actually seen the sharp contrasts.

Every child should have that privilege: the eye-opening, soul-expanding experience of knowing people who are different. From that exposure comes the freedom to accept others.

Parents have within their power the authority to say, "Don't play with the children across the street," or they can say, "Go ahead, play with them, and have fun." Within those two attitudes we instill a spirit in our children that could last them all their lives.

Taking Me to the Game— Just the Two of Us

The crowning dignity of life is to know you are an important individual and there is no one like you. Wealthy is the person who grows up knowing that someone thinks he or she is special. Poor is the person who is always treated as a possession, someone to be calculated and dealt with.

Any parent who has taken their child on a date knows the value of individual attention. Whether it is a camping trip or going to the donut shop, a child's face lights up with the understanding that one parent wants to spend time with him or her—*just the two of them*. If the child has siblings, he or she also likes to do things with them—but for this magical time the individual is selected by a parent to wear the golden slipper. And for a day or an evening that slipper won't fit anyone else's foot.

No one wants to feel like child number two. The

thought is too degrading to grasp. For any person to believe that a parent prefers another sibling is unsettling and brings feelings of insecurity. While he or she may hesitantly admit that the parent likes the other child better, in the young person's heart he or she screams that it is not the case.

Have you ever attempted to take two children on a date only to have one get sick or find an excuse not to go? I have watched our children bail out of group dates from the time they were six until well into their twenties. They longed for the one-on-one, the concentrated effort, the message that says, "I care about *you*."

Children is a category, while *child* is a person. Everyone needs to be more than just one of the children.

No One Can Take Your Place

What would happen if you didn't go home tonight? And what if you never went home again? Would your family simply fill in the space, throw your old shoes out and go on as if nothing had happened? Each of us hopes we would be missed.

Children share that need. They want to know that if they failed to arrive home tonight, no one could ever take their place. There won't be another little Johnny or another Susie. Although there may be other children, no one can ever fill the heart-space that he or she occupies.

Many children sense the fact that their parents are sorry they bore them, are sad that they have to put up with them, and will be overjoyed when they leave the home. Some children imagine they are trouble to their parents, while others have been told so. They have heard some strong statements like:

"It takes a lot to feed someone like you."

"I'll be glad when you grow up."

"I sacrifice plenty for you kids."

Parents may want to get a point across, but they overkill in the process. As a child once said, "I know what your idea of a good time is; it's to get rid of the kids." And the child was correct.

Children should be made to feel that they are like an arm to a parent. To lose that child is to amputate a vital part of the parent, and that part cannot grow back.

Enjoy Their Individual Qualities

Desperate for child-raising strategies, we found the count system described in a book by Charlie Shedd. The scheme was that if a child refused to obey, the parent simply said, "You have the count of three to get that done." The parent didn't say what the punishment would be; he or she simply started counting slowly.

With Mary and Jim the count system worked flawlessly. One of us would say, "That's enough; you have three to get to your chores." On the count of one they would start complaining. "I can't find my shoes," or "Where are my books?" Dutifully we continued to count. On three both of them were ghosts.

Then we had June. She showed considerable independence even from the hospital nursery.

One evening, when she was three years old, June refused to go to bed and I immediately thought of our foolproof scheme. "All right, June," I declared. "You have three to get to your room. One . . ."

June felt for the wall behind her and backed closer to it. Undaunted, I barked, "Two."

As the word left my lips, June spread her legs in a crouched stance and brought both hands up to make fists. Her posture said, "Come on, Pop, take me if you can."

June taught us that children aren't made with cookie cutters. God doesn't bake them on gigantic pans and send them out by the dozen. Mary and Jim would demonstrate no less individuality on different occasions.

Soon we learned not to try to make them comply with each other. Not only did they have a right to be themselves, but they had an overwhelming need to grow in their own way, at their own pace.

If God can make billions of stars, and grains of sand, and snowflakes, and each can have its individual characteristics, surely He creates children with their own identities. Foolishly we have tried to stamp out their personalities rather than choose to love their unique traits.

The child who can never please his parents grows to adulthood with a tremendous sense of inadequacy. The young person will have trouble accepting him or herself when the message is clear: You are unacceptable.

We know that God created everyone with a set of fingerprints, palm prints, footprints, voice prints—even one's own DNA. If such minute individualism does not frighten God, neither should individual personalities rattle us.

Listening Bestows Honor

Children learn quickly that this is an adult world, a kingdom in which children are graded on behavior. If they *do* as they are told, children are promised a life with fewer hassles. What a child thinks, values, feels, dreams, hopes, fears or imagines becomes of little importance. We are task-controlled and if children are to be accepted, they need to complete the tasks assigned them.

I asked a large number of children's workers how they discovered what the children were thinking. After considerable discussion they agreed that they didn't create situations where children could express themselves. Rather, the children's workers designed programs to dazzle the children, and the child's contribution was to sit up straight and not physically accost the child sitting in front of them.

Many of us are uncomfortable talking to our own children. After we ask them how school was and whether they are playing ball, the conversation quickly tapers off. Seldom do we ask how they feel or what is important to them.

Children have opinions, experiences, ideals. Often they long for an adult to suggest that their insight might have some merit. Children have a strong sense of what is fair and unfair, what is honest and dishonest, what is phony and real. Frequently their observations are less cluttered and political than those of adults. Parents can learn a great deal from a child's view of war and hunger, love and hate, hope and despair.

The generation of people who are parents today are products of the blank-slate concept of childhood. This notion taught that children had little to offer, while parents and teachers were responsible for writing both knowledge and feelings on the child's blank mind and psyche. A limited concept of children, this view caused us to neglect the unique contributions children have to offer.

Every person is honored when asked to express his or her thoughts, feelings, and opinions, and the person who asks waits to hear their answer. We show respect and confirm worth by listening to the other person's responses. If we interrupt or ignore, we designate that person as worthless.

Not long ago Bill Moyers, a public television journalist, interviewed an accomplished educator on public television. She said school teachers need to use the knowledge and resources that each child brings to class. Moyers replied that it had never occurred to him that *the child* brings something to the class.

Try observing an adult talking to a child. When another adult enters the room, the adult will usually abruptly end the conversation with the child and begin an entirely new subject with the other adult. He or she clearly does not consider time with the child as valuable as an adult conversation. Just as one would cut off dialogue with a parrot, this person shows rejection to the child.

Accept Children As Divine Gifts

Every child should have the opportunity to hear a significant adult look him or her in the eyes and say with meaning, "I believe you are a special gift from God." No matter what the background or circumstances; regardless of whether the child was adopted, planned or a total surprise. Every child needs to know that someone accepts him or her as a present straight from heaven.

Later when walls start to close in, when children wonder about their individual value, those words need to echo in the chamber of their soul. *There is an adult who believes I am worth something because God has His hand on me.* When life begins to feel empty, those words will supply an inner strength.

Eventually we must watch our teenagers leave to stand on their own. Some depart quickly, others slowly, and some are yo-yos who go in and out, up and down.

Nevertheless, teenagers seem to tie their individuality to their bedroom at home. As long as the bedroom remains relatively the same, they feel there is a safe place to come back to. But with each step, the teen moves out of the bedroom for longer periods of time. He or she is transferring individualism to another nest. It's scary business, but eventually the transition happens. Their personality is finally planted in another place outside their parents' residence. Soon the room is rearranged, turned into a sewing room or the parents move to another house.

Total separation from the young person's room symbolizes the independence to become his or her own person. If their individuality has been both respected and nurtured, teenagers are grateful for parents who gave them dignity and honor. The child was treated as a person with all the privileges that affords.

A Father's Personal Attention

Millions of children suffer because their fathers have simply vanished. A survey suggests that nearly one third of divorced fathers never see their adult children again. It must be hard to feel like a special person if your father chooses to erase you from his life.

By contrast, look at the father in Mark 9:17, who brought his son to Jesus Christ. The boy couldn't speak, foamed at the mouth, and ground his teeth. An evil spirit controlled his body and sent him into convulsions.

What parent can't picture this father, carrying his boy in his arms, hoping against hope that this unusual man can heal his son? He has already been to the disciples and struck out there. Refusing to give up, he presses forward to meet Jesus himself. Imagine the tired look in the father's eyes as he forces himself to dream one more time.

After the father has survived all these obstacles, Jesus Christ tells the man that part of the healing process depends on the father's faith. Listen to the father as he tries desperately to squeeze out enough faith to save his son. He says, "I do believe; help me overcome my unbelief!" (Mark 9:24)

As I read the story I wondered whom he'd left at home. In all probability he had other children whom he loved. But today, for this hour, his terribly sick son was his major focus. Whatever he had to do for this child he was prepared to do. This boy was the most important person in the world at this moment. Someday his son would realize how much he meant to his dad.

Cornhusker Football

We used to scrounge up tickets to watch the University of Nebraska football games. Big Red football is as exciting as life gets where I live. The two favorite pastimes are watching corn grow and going to Memorial Stadium in Lincoln. That explains why on six Saturdays a year the stadium becomes the third largest city in Nebraska.

Each season we tried to locate five tickets so the entire family could go together. Normally during the game Jim and I would be riveted to each play and, of course, to the half-time performances.

The women in our family went along to the games with enthusiasm, but their attention span was limited. They were content to spend most of the three hours eating peanuts, chatting, and watching balloons fly away. That was fine with me. I felt like Super Dad hustling my family off to the biggest event on Nebraska's cultural calendar.

One Saturday I was able to dislodge only two football tickets from my usual sources. For whatever reason, I went to nine-year-old June and asked her if she would go to the ball game with me all by herself. Her eyes lit up at once.

When the time came, June buckled up in the front seat of our old Buick and we tooled out onto Interstate 80 and headed for Lincoln. She talked the entire trip and waved at neighbors and friends.

The two of us cheered, chatted, chanted and roared at the game. Afterward we stopped to eat and talked about what we liked most at the stadium.

For one Saturday a fourth-grader became Queen of the Plains. Her father gave her his undivided attention (except for six or seven touchdowns). June knew she was special because her father told her so— not just with words, but also by his actions.

Years later when June wrote home from college, she mentioned the day in Lincoln with "just my dad and me."

Sometimes we go to an extreme and make our children the center of our lives. Two adults stop everything for the sake of their children's activities. The danger exists that too much constant attention gives children the feeling that the universe revolves around them. Like overwatered plants, children will benefit from some apathy.

But they need to know they are special in someone's eyes (hopefully in two or more people's hearts).

A crying child with messy diapers who is throwing food may not seem like a gift from heaven, but it's true. If you doubt it, ask a couple who can't have a child. They understand fully that a child is a blessing from God. Smart parents tell each child that he or she is a special package from above. "Sons are a heritage from the Lord, children a reward from him" (Ps. 127:3).

Stripping Gears and Denting Fenders

When a child begins to climb trees, parents face one of their most difficult decisions. Will they stick around and forbid the child to explore God's monkey bars? Or has the time come for the parents to retreat silently into the house and wait patiently with hands clenched tightly in prayer? Bravely they listen for a loud thud and a woeful cry for Mom.

Much like fishing, we all wonder when to let out more line and when to pull our catch closer to the boat. Let them run; hold them close; let them try; keep them safe.

The answer is complex because there are many variables. It depends on who the child is and who the parent is and what the circumstances might be. That isn't what we like to hear. We would like to know that 8.5 is the right age to go to the pool alone, or 10.75 is the age to camp out with the neighbor kids.

Unfortunately, letting go is an art, a picture each family must paint for itself, and no two scenes will look the same.

We can count on at least one result: Both the children who are released too soon and the children who are released too late seem to resent it. Being overprotective and being non-protective are both bummers. A bartender in a university town in Kansas said he gets both kinds: The rabble-rousers are those who either grew up in strict homes that allowed no freedom, or wide-open homes that permitted anything and everything.

Those two extremes are also prone to produce shy children. A child who is coddled suffers from a lack of experience, and those who are encouraged to try everything are overwhelmed by life's challenges. The happy middle is hard to find but well worth the search.

The Teacher's Plants

Some of the finest people who daily touch the lives of young people are teachers. Several have been highly influential and inspirational in my life. One still remains for me as the teacher who thoughtlessly inflicted pain and insecurity.

It was the last day of school and my sixth-grade teacher was taking her plants home for the summer. She had asked a few of us to help carry them to her car.

I enthusiastically agreed to help, but as an awkward adolescent, I was always stumbling over my feet or bumping into doorjambs. As I returned from making a trip to the car, I entered the classroom hurriedly and banged into a desk. There in front of me stood the teacher holding her last plant. I reached out for the prize but she drew it back. Looking behind me she said, "Here, Freddie, you take this one," and she handed the plant to the boy behind me.

Decades later, I still remember that teacher. She had been one of my favorites. I also remember the crummy plant. When I feel down on myself and a bit inadequate, I still find myself wishing she had handed me that plant. I might have dropped it, but I wish she would have given me the chance to try.

Wheels Change Everything

Most parents have at least one horror story to tell about their children's experiences with the automobile. A driver's license causes one of the most severe changes in a parent/child relationship. In the early teen years, a struggle goes on over how much freedom to allow the child. A driver's license catapults the young person over the wall and leaves parents shaking with fear.

The first time a teenager drives the car "away" from home, parents sink into nervous despair. It's hard enough that the child should be allowed to drive the family peacefully to church and to the Happy Hamburger Restaurant afterward, but the thought of him or her driving *alone,* or worse yet, with other teenagers, is overwhelming.

The first time Mary drove the car by herself to Lincoln (75 miles away) caused enough tension to make my gums ache. We had her practice changing a tire before allowing her to sample the super highway, but that did little to ease our minds. Our oldest girl, the baby who not so long ago rested peacefully in the crook of my arm, would be all alone on the asphalt avenues of life. At any moment this naive babe could be swindled, deceived, stolen, and crushed in an evil world.

Pat and I paced, fretted, prayed, and twitched until we finally heard the old jalopy rattle back into the driveway. When Mary reappeared in the house, we acted like it was no big deal and we hadn't even given the adventure a thought. (Mary found that hard to believe since we'd asked her to stop and call home twice along the way.)

Almost every parent dies this death. Such is our fate. Our calling is to let go with one hand while we clench a fist in anxiety with the other.

Nervously we say dumb things like:

"Be careful."
"Don't play the radio; you'll be distracted."
"Don't talk while you drive."
"Be sure the doors are locked."
"Watch the brakes, you could chip a tooth."

In contrast, we rarely say:

"Have a good time."
"Air out the carburetor."
"Don't hurry home."
"Take plenty of friends along."

The pressures of holding your child back and setting him or her free all rush in at once. How will you know what is right and what isn't? Your best bet is to aim for the middle. If a fender gets smashed, pray it won't be two. If your insurance goes up, just hope you don't have to use it too often or you could lose it altogether.

The teenager is almost as frightened as the parent. But both realize that letting go has to happen. Later, when the young person looks back, he or she will realize how courageous and generous you were to allow driving privileges at all.

The ease of present-day driving makes you wonder how our parents ever put up with a stick shift. Our newest car is a GLC Mazda with a stick. I thought it would be fun for all of us to learn a new adventure, so I purchased a manual transmission with that in mind.

Our first two children took to the controls like veterans of the Indy 500. However, June perceived it more as a rodeo than a racing event.

I remember sitting next to her as she ground through the gears. The little charcoal sedan bucked, lurched, snorted, and died. Each time, I reassured her that she was doing a great job and she should turn the key and try again. Determined, she revved up the engine and soon we were riding along in a highway blender—tossed from side to side, from top to floor.

Her brother and sister warned me that June shouldn't be allowed to drive that car because the clutch wouldn't last. But we were building memories, and doing aerobics at the same time.

Experiences like this make us wonder if God has anxiety attacks, too, as He watches His children grow. Our potential for both good and evil is considerable, and God must wonder which we will most frequently choose. But despite our propensity for evil, God still lets us live in the neighborhood of life. He doesn't box us in or keep us grounded. As a loving parent, He chooses to let us make our own mistakes. Through parenting, we catch a glimpse of how hard some of those decisions may have been for God to make. I'm thankful He's opted to let us drive the stick shift and bounce the car around the block for ourselves.

Protection From Pain

Loving parents try to keep their children from pain. That's understandable, but it is also regrettable. All of us need the scuffed knees and bruised egos that go with growing up. Children learn coping skills and adjust to setbacks if they are allowed to face situations for themselves.

I once saw a mother stop her car abruptly and jump out to confront some children standing on a street corner.

"You both know that you are ignoring my Angie at school," she barked. "If you wanted to, you could be her friend. How would you feel if the other kids mistreated you?"

It's easy to appreciate how that mother felt and what she was trying to do, but what good did it accomplish? She wanted to alleviate her daughter's pain, but in the final analysis she probably created more agony for her.

The strong parenting instinct to protect our children can blind us to common sense. They have to climb the tree, take the wheel, swing on the rope, go on a date, try out for the team, and go to school without a jacket. Pain has to become part of their experience if they are ever to recognize, and appreciate, pleasure. Defeat is part of the package if they are ever to see victory. Rejection has to be part of the mix in order to sift out acceptance.

We never quite get over trying to protect everyone. Not long ago Pat's Aunt Nell came to visit us. She is in her early 80s and has been retired from school-teaching for some time.

On a summer evening we invited Nell to come with us and watch us hit fly balls, a ritual we have observed for years. We took along a lawn chair and tried to make her comfortable while we chased balls across the field.

After a few minutes of boredom, Nell abandoned her chair and asked if she could take a turn at bat. She hit several fly balls and soon insisted on playing the outfield. Sportively she chased down ground balls and tossed them back to the pitcher as if she were a schoolgirl.

The protection business is risky and should be practiced sparingly for all ages. Although all of us need it at some time, prolonged or inappropriate protection is never appreciated. What adult has ever said, "I'm glad my parents overprotected me"?

Some parents buy toys so intricate and expensive that they dare not let their children play with them. Some purchase homes beside beautiful parks and refuse to let their children roam among the trees. Wise parents allow scuffed knees, while they wait in the background with the bandages ready.

The Steady Move Toward Freedom

Fortunate are the young people whose parents gave them more freedom with each passing year. Thankful are those who were allowed to sail for themselves, yet knew they had a dependable harbor.

The question is repeatedly asked, "When do we cut our children loose and allow them to become adults?" The answer is to release them gradually in a steady move toward freedom. If this is consistent, they will have less trouble separating from us after high school.

The Dilapidated Apartment

When our children left home they were quite adept at making their own decisions. They decided if they would attend school, which school they would attend, and where they would live. Sometimes they asked advice, but not often.

This open policy was sorely tested when June selected an apartment in a shadowy part of Lincoln. She picked it out, made the deposit, collected a couple of roommates and moved in. Soon after, she invited us to come see her place and bring along some of her possessions from home.

Before I made the trip, I asked a couple of my friends what the neighborhood was like. "No problem," they assured me. "There aren't nearly as many murders on those streets as there used to be."

When Pat and I drove to June's street, the word that was impressed on us was "lurking." Dark doorways, unlighted parks, overgrowth everywhere. People stood around on the streets without any apparent purpose or destination.

Tall bushes hugged the building. We walked hesitantly into the foyer of the apartment house. No lights brightened the entrance. We didn't feel safe— and it was daytime.

June showed us her quarters and we nearly fainted. The back door frame was shattered where someone had previously kicked in the door from the outside.

"No problem," June said, smiling. "The landlord said he would fix the door and put on an extra lock."

"That would be helpful," I mumbled in disbelief. "Nice place."

I drove home that evening in a state of shock. All night I couldn't sleep. I worried, I paced, I prayed, I fantasized. It would be only a matter of time before the police would call and ask me to come and identify the body. I knew it would happen and yet I managed to keep it all inside.

One night, cycling home from school, June was confronted by a man. Later she told me it was "hairy," but she "handled" the situation. She has never said what "hairy" and "handled" meant.

After June moved out to share a safer apartment with her sister, I told her how I had felt about the seedy place she had left. June said with relief, "I'm so glad you didn't say anything. I was under so much pressure. Between picking a place and getting everyone moved in, I couldn't have stood it if you had come in at the last minute and shot me down."

It was just like Jim climbing trees and Mary driving her first car. When do you back off and when do you speak up? And how do parents stop from going mad as they let their children go?

We have a Heavenly Father who gives us the freedom to find out for ourselves. He doesn't keep us in a bubble and He doesn't guarantee our tomorrows. Sometimes He just says "nice place" and lets us make our own choices.

Telling Me to Call Collect

Communication is tough.

Half the time we aren't sure how we feel about love and fear and disappointment and hope and despair. How do we verbalize what we don't understand? How do we reach deep into our hearts and communicate what is going on inside?

Add to that the problem of whom to tell anyway. If we locate our feelings as best we understand them, is there anyone who will sit still long enough to hear us out? Does anyone actually care what is stored in the locker of our emotions?

These are the questions that young people struggle with. Does anyone want to hear about it? Teenagers would like to know that their parents are good and caring listeners. When they need to talk, on their time schedule and according to their emotional clock, will their parents be willing to give the attention they need?

Young people complain that (number one) their parents don't understand. And (number two) they don't listen. Most of us as parents have performed according to these statements at some time. The accusation isn't totally groundless. Thankful is the youth who feels his or her parents at least try in these two areas.

In an attempt to keep his teenage son out of trouble, a father repeatedly said, "If you get into trouble, young man, don't you come to me." The son believed him. When he had difficulties with the law or alcohol or his car or his peers, the boy never called home. He didn't need the added rejection of his father.

When he drank too much, the boy drove around all night until he felt sober. When he crashed the car, he didn't call to ask his father for help. All the lines of communication had been cut by a well-intentioned father.

What if the father had said, "You are responsible for any trouble you get into; but if I can ever give you a ride, just call me." That message speaks of responsibility and open communication. Instead, the father drove home a point and drove his son away.

Wiser parents give their teenager a quarter and say, "If anything happens, call me." The invitation is wide open. A security net is spread in case they fall.

He Knew He Could Call Home

During his early teen years, our son Jim was hanging around a bad situation one evening and I heard about it. Anxiously I drove to the area. I spotted Jim and motioned him over to my car. When he got in, his expression showed his obvious relief.

"You know, you could have called me," I said as we drove off.

Jim replied simply, "I know."

The words "I know" sent goosebumps up my spine. He knew he could count on me. Somehow I had managed to get that message across. He didn't call, but that was secondary. Jim knew he could.

In the story of the prodigal son (Luke 15), the son knew he could call home. He didn't want to call, and he didn't until he was feeding pigs and starving, but he knew he could. When he ran out of everything, including pride, he went home to a father who ran to him and hugged and kissed him. Did the son feel thankful? I think he had gratitude gushing out of his pores.

What's the point of calling if you know your parent will brush you off like attic dust? Parents need to make it as painless as possible for their child to call. Teenagers need to know they won't get chewed out when they call. The next day the parent might rant, rave, and ground them until Halley's Comet returns. But tonight it's a rescue mission. Bring them home and serve hot chocolate.

Collect Calls—a Blessing From God

When the monthly phone bills arrive, collect calls seem like an invention of Satan. You figure it's his way of wrecking the national economy as well as your own financial life. But on the night when your teenager calls, choked up and anxious, you know collect calls were created by a committee of wise angels.

Fortunately, that's how God's telephone system works, too. Day or night we can call Him collect. The bill is paid in full and He is always glad to hear from us. Though He always appreciates good news, He also wants to help out with the bad.

Earthly parents aren't exactly like our Heavenly Parent, but it's a great place to start. If I call God in the middle of the night, will He refuse to accept the charges? The thought is too frightening to contemplate.

Simply put, the Bible reminds us, "The Lord will hear when I call to him" (Ps. 4:3).

That's part of our safety net. Our children need no less.

How many children have we heard say, "If I told my father that, he would kill me"? Some are saying that their father will be harsh and mean. Other children know better. Though they expect their parent to be upset, they also expect to get a good hearing. It doesn't bother them that their parent will feel strongly about the incident; the parent probably should. But first and foremost the parent will care and listen.

The Midnight Call

Imagine that you get a call late at night from your teenage son (collect, of course). He's been in an accident and he needs you. Immediately a galaxy of thoughts races through your mind. The thoughts will probably include:

> Are you all right? How much is this call going to cost? Was there much damage? My hair's too messy to be seen in public. It's past your curfew. I've got to get up early in the morning. Do you have the good car?

The test is, which thoughts will come first? Don't be terribly surprised if some of your thoughts are out of order. If your hand dashes directly to the top of your head, you know it's concern over your hair. If you look quickly toward the bed, you are wishing your spouse had answered the phone. If your eyes dart toward the clock, you are probably thinking of the violated curfew.

Most parents instantly give the correct response. "Are you all right?" You still have your priorities intact.

Be reassured, the collect call means your teenagers are thankful you never said things like:

"If you get pregnant, don't bring it home."

"If you get in trouble with the police, consider yourself on your own."

"If you're drinking, don't call me."

"If you have problems, let your squirrelly friends help you."

Parents may feel like saying something along these lines, but smart parents think it over. If you haven't already, someday thank God for all the things you thought but refused to say. God may have quickly flooded your brain with good sense. All of us say enough dumb things; we ought to be grateful for the remarks we manage to swallow.

Midnight calls require clear thinking and genuine compassion. It's easier to say the right thing if we already feel the right way. When our first and major concern is for the safety of our child, we are far more likely to show that with our first or second response.

Back to the story of the prodigal son. When the son did return home, what was the father's major concern?

"Where is the money?"

"I told you so."

"Don't come home smelling like a pig sty."

"Well, I hope you've learned your lesson, young man."

"I hope you didn't get anyone pregnant."

None of the above. The father was all hugs and kisses. He welcomed him with open arms, accepted him, forgave him, and called for a celebration. What he may have discussed with the boy later, we can't be sure. But we do know that he got love across immediately.

Are your children like our children? They have called home collect when:

They wrecked the car.

They were away for the summer.

They broke up with a friend.

They wrecked the car.

They wanted to drop out of school.

They were pitifully lonely.

They needed a ride.

They wrecked the car.

They wanted us to make it all right.

They needed money.

They wanted to strangle a teacher.

They wrecked the car.

They needed to cry.

They wanted to celebrate.

They wrecked the car.

If you read the list carefully, you may discover a pattern. Or maybe it just seemed like one. What's important is that they knew they could call, and they knew we would listen.

Most of us carry a credit card in case we need instant help. We have bank cards, telephone cards, and medical insurance cards because we see them as safety nets. Young people like to know that the warm voice of a parent is their safety net at any hour of the day or night.

As Christians, we know the only total security is found in Jesus Christ. Ultimately, in the light of eternity, only Christ can right all the wrongs. But during those changing years of adolescence, parents serve as a reflection of the security Christ provides.

Feel Free to Talk

The freedom to call means children don't need to hide. They don't expect their parents to refuse to accept the charges. Neither do they expect their parents to reject them or call them names or make them feel like fools.

One of the saddest scenes I have seen on television was one in which a runaway girl called home. Her mother answered the phone, but her father refused to talk to her. This young girl quickly vanished back into the darkness of a big, ugly city.

Young people who believe they will be heard are likely to talk to their parents. If they think they will be shut down and shut off, teenagers are not likely to bring up uncomfortable subjects.

A young girl told her parents that she didn't agree with their views on premarital sex. She was straightforward, honest, and even gentle. In return, her parents extended the same courtesy. They reminded her of what they believed was important and valuable.

No screaming. No shock treatment. No ultimatums. No personal condemnation. Everyone acted like civil, caring people. Because her parents didn't condemn her for her viewpoint, that girl was free to change her mind and even later agree with her parents. If there had been an ugly scene over the issue, the teenager would most likely have kept her views to herself and more strongly resisted her parents' values.

An open line means both accessibility and tolerance.

There are some things teenagers feel uncomfortable about discussing with their parents. But the greater the amount of openness, the greater the possibility of communication. If teens sense a put-down, they are less likely to approach their parents with a problem.

Communication is difficult under the best of circumstances. When it is further exasperated by age difference, diverse opinions, teenage subculture, separate experiences, and growing individuality, communication takes extra work. Many parents attempt to enter into dialogue with their teenagers and within two minutes invariably break into an argument. Soon one of them stomps out of the room, both sides frustrated and angry.

Keep trying. Even if you don't succeed, your children will remember that you tried. They will understand that the two of you stood on opposite banks of the river looking desperately for a bridge over which you could cross and find each other. It's great if you can discover the bridge. But almost as good is the knowledge that both of you were searching for it.

God doesn't want to hear from me only when I am behaving well. He doesn't want me to call only when I agree with what's going on. When I am confused, rebellious, feeling insecure and lost, God wants me to call upon Him. I don't think He will hang up on me or refuse to accept the charges.

To Fight for Justice—and Still Chill Out

While abortion issues were red hot and tempers were flaring, Mary picked up a placard and stood on a street corner. She wanted someone to hear her heart-cry. The words were printed on cardboard, but the passion behind those words voiced a deep commitment to justice.

Maybe some of her friends wouldn't appreciate her stand, or perhaps her bosses didn't agree with what she was doing, but that was the risk Mary had to take. She wanted people to like her, but beyond the need for acceptance this graduate student had to stand up for what she believed was right.

No doubt she received her sense of justice from the battles waged within her own soul. As often as not, Mary disagrees with her parents over what's right and what should be done about it. But she does feel the freedom to reach her own conclusions and stand up for them in her own way.

Those are two freedoms for which young adults

can be tremendously grateful. First, the encouragement to weigh their own sense of right and wrong.
Second, the liberty to express their values in the way
they see best.

Parents often attempt to cage their children's
value systems. Afraid to let them make choices,
adults work hard to control their youngsters' minds.
As a result, we frequently end up with bitter young
adults who lash out to express their sense of justice
and injustice.

Rather than dictate the agenda, we might be
smarter to grant permission to stand up for convic-
tions. The child will be forever thankful for the lear-
ner's permit that says he or she is free to try. When
the sense of justice comes as a message from the
Spirit of God, the grown child will then be more apt
to accept it as a mission.

Frustration results when parents require that their
children speak out on certain prescribed issues. Joy
results when children have been encouraged to
"work out their own salvation."

We know a mother who constantly complained
because her son was not involved in missions. She
dropped hints the size of a locomotive. She fretted
and jabbed in hopes that he would choose to fulfill
her agenda. Harassed, he was determined never to do
anything even remotely related to missions. He refused to give her a moment's consolation.

This mother created an impasse by denying her
son the freedom to follow Christ for himself. Today,
he doesn't even trust the Holy Spirit. He's afraid it's
only the echo of his nagging mother.

Let Justice Come Naturally

There is a vast difference between permission and
pressure, or allowing our child to do something and

pressuring him or her to do something. That difference explains why our children frequently do the exact opposite of what their parents desperately want them to do or not do. Children perceive the pressure as an attempt to enslave them. Often parents desire to live out their lives through their children. Today's children are smart enough to recognize that—and they reject it.

If they do receive their sense of justice from their parents, they must acquire it naturally. It must filter down to them, not be crammed down their throats.

Some of the saddest statements are, "I became a minister to please my powerful aunt," or "I went to the mission field because my parents always expected it of me." The Christian countryside is dotted with disillusioned wrecks who tried hard to make their parents' dreams come true.

We begin with the premise that justice is an integral part of both the Old and the New Testaments. Isaiah promised us that the Messiah would bring justice to the nations (Isa. 51:5), and Matthew reminded us of that also: "He [Jesus] will proclaim justice to the nations" (12:18). Justice must play an important part in the experience and expression of every Christian.

"But what if it doesn't filter down to our children?" is the worry of many Christian parents. If children don't see it in us and model after us of their own volition, it will never be part of them anyway. When parents force values on their children, those values only become attachments. They never become part of the child's core. We all know that, yet most of us push for compliance anyway.

A young girl spoke at a convention I attended. Everyone was thrilled at her presentation. But two things were troublesome to me. One, the vocabulary was not her own. Two, the theme that she so passionately addressed was not her experience. Obviously her parents had helped her learn the words and emote them effectively. The cause had been *attached* to her life. As a spectator I had to wonder where that kind of manipulation eventually leads.

Where do we draw the line between child involvement and unhealthy manipulation? Children who later feel used often rebel against the very cause that their parents pushed so hard.

There is a man in the Midwest who grew up with missionary parents. His family was captured by the Japanese and years later returned to the United States. As a teenager he witnessed about Christ in both the concentration camp and on the return voyage home. Today, as an aging adult, this same person wants nothing to do with the Gospel of Jesus Christ.

The question worth asking is whether the witnessing was ever his idea. Was it ever part of his fiber or spirit? Was he perhaps programmed by his environment and his parents to carry out a function of which he never truly became a part?

We can't demand a sense of justice. We can't "wire" our children for compassion. First, the example must be supplied by caring parents, and second we must be content to let the Holy Spirit work in our children's hearts. It is often difficult for parents to rely on those two resources. We still want to give an added push.

Every three or four months a little girl knocks on my office door. She is a sweet and polite child who sells cookies to help support a church in a neighboring town. Going door to door, she solicits while her mother stays outside in the car.

To me, the girl is a depressing sight: controlled, manipulated, and unaware of how much she is being used. Is this her idea or will she wake up someday to see herself as a victim? Will she one day be angry at God and her mother? The potential appears to be there.

The temptation is to feel that because children are apparently too young to understand the need for justice and involvement, they must be put to work. It is argued that later they will grow to appreciate what they are doing. There may be some grain of truth to this, but the risk is their reaction when they discover that they were used as a pawn in someone else's chess game.

A Convict in Our Home

No one would confuse us with the great prison reformers of history, but we did have a convict in our home for five days. Kevin was part of a work project and came to our community to help paint a house for a needy family.

Though Kevin hadn't committed a violent crime, his presence made us more than a little nervous. My main concern was whether or not to lock our bedroom door at night. If I did lock it, should I also tell the children to lock theirs? Or should I simply keep up my macho image and then secretly lock the door while the children were left vulnerable in the case of a crazed midnight attack?

It proved a great crisis of faith. Was I a bold disciple of Christ or a wimpy Christian hiding in my bedroom? Had I exposed my family to a deadly situation or somehow opened their lives to the possibility of accepting other people, regardless of their past?

As Jim and Kevin talked, I wondered what kind of influence they might have on each other. My son was learning from a convicted felon who professed to be a Christian; but we didn't know exactly *what* Jim was learning.

Some people in the town didn't like our bringing prisoners into the community and said so. Many others supported the project wholeheartedly. There are no apparent lingering bad feelings over the action, but we wondered what effect it would have on our children because of the controversy and misunderstanding it caused.

We concluded that such exposure could only be helpful. A bit of controversy couldn't hurt anyone; everyone must learn to become comfortable with ill winds blowing. The children weren't being used nor were they expected to take direct responsibility for their parents' actions. And no one was maimed, robbed, or beheaded during the night.

Basically, Pat and I are reluctant to rush into unsettled situations. Most of our calls for justice are sent through the mail. They end up being noted on some heartless legislative computer or virtually ignored. Our risk factor is usually limited to postage and a creative sentence or two. However, the occasional foray into the arena of justice helps awaken the senses to the world around us. It also tells the family there is life beyond video games.

Example is probably the best training tool. Children need to see rather than merely hear about our concepts of correct behavior. They also need to know where our passions lie, no matter how imperfect those passions might be.

"Train a child in the way he should go, and when he is old he will not turn from it" (Prov. 22:6).

Justice Without Neuroses

At some point in their lives most children become perfectionists. That may be hard to believe if you have a teenager, but the perfectionist stage comes and goes. For some children the phase lasts for years and in a few cases they never fully come out of it.

While they play with the need to be perfect (somewhere between 11 and 30) the concept of justice can become overwhelming. Because the needs of humankind worldwide are endless, many young people become morbidly concerned over the terrible conditions in the world. When they go over the edge and become "guilt stricken," they may need the help of a parent to come back to reality.

We knew of a couple whose teenage daughter became emotionally paralyzed over the needs of the world. She soon lost her sense of humor and saw everything as stern and crucial. If she saw her parents eating lettuce, she went into her labor-relations speech. Before long they were unable to throw a soft drink can away, buy popcorn at a theater, or mention *mankind* without getting a lecture on social relevance. She saw nothing as funny, light, or enjoyable anymore. Life was extremely serious.

Partly out of their own need to survive, and partly out of concern for their daughter, the parents decided to intervene. One evening at the dinner table as their daughter began to espouse another cause, her mother told her flatly to cool it. She explained to her daughter that she had gone too far; it was past time to chill out. The worst thing she could lose was her sense of humor. Being uptight for Christ wasn't to anyone's advantage.

From that day on their daughter began to live a more balanced life. Justice and mercy remained strong concerns, but now they were accented with a proper dose of lightheartedness. Later the girl said that she appreciated her mother's intervention, and acknowledged that it was a turning point for her. Zeal must be tempered with an even outlook.

Often we meet people who are overburdened with

shoulds and *oughts.* They probably grew up in an environment where they were fed a daily diet of strict obligation. Wound tightly and fitted to a mold, they become like Martha in Luke 10, who couldn't lay down duty and enjoy a full life.

Bless your children with a thirst for justice, but do not curse them with an insatiable sense of guilt.

Charity Without a Chip on Its Shoulder

Young adults who grow up in "burdened" households tend to become highly judgmental of others. They are intense about everything, and can't understand why others aren't as committed as they are. Consequently, if they are concerned for the homeless or the lost, they can't understand why everyone doesn't share an equal concern. Others are judged by their own standards and come up woefully lacking.

How many young people (or older, for that matter) return from short-term mission assignments or an inner-city ministry angry at, or at least critical of, everyone else for their lack of involvement? I have no official survey, but it seems like a micro-chip full. They want to know why everyone isn't praying at 5:00 A.M., or why we sit idly watching television, or why we don't sell everything we have and give to the poor, or move out of our comfortable homes. They are angry at the world and carry a chip on their shoulders.

Our children will be solidly grateful if we release them from attitudes of judgment and hostility. If we raise them to be moral policemen, we condemn them to a path of frustration and alienation. Free your children from the burning fire of attitudes that threaten to consume them.

If we can model a balanced life of compassion and

justice with joy, our children will hopefully come to recognize it as a life they want for themselves. Compassion without joy is a wheel without tires, making the journey terribly rough.

Thanks for...

Baptizing Me in the River

All Christian parents want to see their children become Christians. Unfortunately, not everyone will see it happen. But when their children do make that decision, parents feel as if their children have become whole. They have experienced the most important change they will ever know.

Angels rejoice in heaven when a child accepts Christ, and parents dance in their hearts for joy. They know that a genuine commitment to Christ is the greatest fulfillment this life has to offer.

But in our enthusiasm to see our children become Christians, are we willing to let them have the experience as their own? Or are we so intense that we program our children so that their experience will be exactly like ours? If a child later feels he was trapped into making a decision that he didn't understand, he may see his Christian life as merely a function to perform rather than a passion to fulfill.

Recently I asked a group of Christians how they

would like to serve Jesus Christ. Of the dozen, not one had any desire to work for Christ. They weren't frustrated disciples—they didn't see themselves as disciples at all.

There is not much life there if a person sees Christian commitment as just another way to please his or her parents. Children are expected to go to college, call home regularly, come back for Thanksgiving, and become Christians.

The reason why so many college students don't attend church during their first year or more on campus is an attempt to declare their independence. They want to prove they can avoid church services and get along just fine. The young people whose parents did not manipulate their decision to follow Christ have less need to defy the norms.

I know of several young people who were forced by their parents to go to Bible College. Feeling controlled and manipulated, they rebelled against the school because they saw it as an extension of their parents' heavy hand. To this day, many of these young persons remain bitter because their parents tried to dictate their spiritual lives.

Declare Independence for Them

Smart parents give their children great latitude in making spiritual choices. They believe their children can have genuine experiences with Christ on their own, even far exceeding their parents' expectations. Their children are given permission to launch out, to communicate with Christ on their own terms.

When June wanted to be baptized at twenty years of age, the choice was hers entirely. Our local church had planned a baptismal service at the river, and I was asked to be a part of her commitment to Christ. Much of my joy came in knowing that it was her own decision to be baptized. She didn't do it to please or impress her parents.

As I stood in the river and baptized my daughter in the name of the Father, the Son, and the Holy Spirit, I was happy that June had made her own choice.

I had previously baptized another of our children, and the third hasn't yet chosen to be baptized. But when that child does decide, it will come from the heart. All three claim a faith in Christ as their Savior, and they "work out" their beliefs in their own ways.

Too many parents chew their fingernails for fear their children will not follow in their spiritual footprints. Afraid they will or won't speak in tongues. Worried that they will or won't get involved. Tormented whether they will attend a church that immerses, sprinkles, pours, dips or sponge bathes.

Some children feel the pressure even into their 30's and 40's, when their parents continue to look over their spiritual shoulders, judging their commitment and Christian witness. It's as though their parents have turned into spiritual parole officers. While they are free adults, they remain tethered to highly judgmental parents who deal out approval or withhold approval with each decision they make.

One father feels satisfied that he gave his children total church freedom. "One of them goes to high church," he explained. "Lots of liturgy, classical music, and they read a lot in the service. Another child attends the Church of the Entirely Laid Back. They meet in a circle and everyone interprets the Scripture as they see fit. The worshipers might wear sandals and jeans. The third child is a satellite Christian. When that one makes it out of bed, she floats around and samples congregations. I don't know if we did it right or wrong, but that's how it turned out."

Inside, I envy those three young people because they are doing it their own way.

Is Commitment to Christ the Real Issue?

Children eventually figure out what their parents consider important. They know if parents are interested in conformity, appearances, church games, commitment, service, or Jesus Christ himself. If parents are playing religious roles, their children may choose to follow that pattern or they may decide to break it.

Each parent does well to ask himself if commitment to Christ is the real issue. Is it our great desire and prayer that our children be one in Christ and be led by the Holy Spirit? If that is the case, we can be less concerned about which liturgy they follow or whether or not they attend the men's prayer breakfast.

Because Christ encourages us not to judge each other, He surely wants that courtesy extended to our children. In order to do that, we have to pull our hands back and let the children "run" with Christ in their own free way. Unfortunately for many Christian parents, *freedom* and *liberty* have become synonymous with evil. By their actions they convey that *conformity, control,* and *compliance* are signs of spirituality. For them it will be difficult to let their children go and follow Christ for themselves.

When to Speak Up

Young adults have told us repeatedly that they don't want advice from their parents unless they ask for it. One person said he refused to do what was right because his parents told him he had to do it. Doesn't that sound like youthful pride and the struggle for independence?

Despite my "spiritual freedom" approach, I remember one night when I clearly intervened and told one of my girls what decision she should make.

Mary had gone off to college, and while there had become involved in a campus ministry. I was well acquainted with the group and understood something about their concept of control. They demanded total obedience to the leadership and didn't stand for much disagreement or individual expression.

I knew Mary wasn't particularly looking for my opinion or blessing. But the group's potential for mind-control and spiritual damage was driving me to panic attacks. They had left many spiritual bodies strewn along the highway and I cringed at the horror stories their victims told me.

When Mary came home for a weekend, I decided to break every child-raising tenet I considered sacred. Late in the evening I sat down with her and asked pointed questions about the group. Then, with agony of soul, I told her what I thought of their tactics and the eventual fallout.

That wouldn't have been hard for some parents, but for me it was a serious conflict of conscience. Was I interfering; was I misdirecting; was I steering her away from a rich spiritual experience? In my heart I believed I was protecting her from a spiritual disaster. It was one of those soul-wrenching decisions that I don't enjoy.

Not immediately, but fairly soon, Mary dropped out of the group. Later she talked about the problems she saw, and how she had changed in ways she didn't like while involved in the group.

There is no general rule for how or when or if a parent should intervene. There is definitely a time to speak up and a time to remain silent. Smart parents select those times carefully and wisely. But if we are going to take a risk, let's interfere as seldom as possible.

Spiritual Adults

Some strong guidance can be found in Galatians 4:1–7. Paul draws the analogy that under the old system we needed the law to act as our guardian and trustee; then Christ redeemed us and gave us full spiritual standing. We are now heirs of God and not slaves to the law.

Spiritual rebirth frees each of us to follow Christ as individuals. Each of us is a priest who has direct access to the Heavenly Father. It would be foolish and harmful to expect our children to remain under our spiritual dictatorship.

We can give our children a double heritage. First, we pass on a spiritual example of belief and commitment to Jesus Christ. Second, we release them to spiritual maturity so they can make their own decisions.

Spiritual Examples

The challenge to be a spiritual example to our children is an awesome responsibility. Parents must realize that a casual Christian example tends to produce casual Christians. Sunday Christians tend to produce Sunday Christians. Those who debate spiritual issues will probably produce debaters, cynics will most likely produce cynics, and those who consistently criticize leadership in the church will produce children who tend to do the same. Thankfully, this isn't always the case.

Probably the most constructive way to influence our children's Christian lives is by leadership. Words of wisdom are not enough, but a life of example can leave an incredible impact.

Paul said it this way: "Follow my example, as I follow the example of Christ" (1 Cor. 11:1).

Parents who work with neglected children, who visit mission fields, who clothe the deprived, who teach special classes, who take risks, who visit prisons, and who pray, are far more likely to reproduce in kind. Those who try to force their children into paths they have not taken themselves end up with disaster.

Whether or not we ever leave a material inheritance, we surely want to pass on a spiritual one. Children may squander a spiritual inheritance just as they may abuse a financial inheritance. However, that should not stop us from passing it down. Even if our spiritual inheritance seems meager and tattered, we can leave them something. Old rocking chairs are popular, quilts are nice, antique cars are a hoot, but a spiritual heritage is priceless.

"I pray also that the eyes of your heart may be enlightened in order that you may know the hope to which he has called you, the riches of his glorious inheritance . . ." (Eph. 1:18).

One of Those

A mother asked her teenage son where he was going. He told her he was off to Bible study. She shot back with contempt, "Oh, my, you aren't going to become one of *those,* are you?"

As he grew, the young man never got over that acid remark. His mother didn't want anything to do with that much spirituality and she didn't want him to have it either.

The Bible study gave him strength. The people in the group showed him warmth and love. All of these added to his confidence and helped give him purpose.

But he can't forget his mother's comment that was burned in his heart three decades ago. Even though she probably didn't realize its impact, he still resents the fact that she disapproved of something that was vitally important to him.

Be careful before you rain on someone else's spiritual parade. Most likely he or she will resent the intrusion.

The Bible appropriately warns us against putting out or quenching the Spirit's fire (1 Thess. 5:19). Drowning the fire in our own lives is bad enough; quenching it in someone else's life is a serious crime.

As parents we watch them leave. They may head out for city ghettos to teach children, or explore the rolling hills of Vermont to organize Vacation Bible Schools; they may even go to another country to serve for a summer, and we know the power of the living Christ goes with them. That should be enough. Give them the freedom to go where the Spirit leads.

Love
and
Dates

When Jerry heard that his father's condition was worsening, he hurried home to Nashville. Cancer had taken its toll, but his father was still coherent.

Sitting beside the hospital bed, Jerry took his aging father's hand and drew close. "Dad, I want you to know that I love you."

"You're a good son," his father replied.

"You hear me, don't you?" the son said passionately. "I want you to know that I love you."

"Keep an eye on your mother for me," the father requested evenly.

Jerry left the room angry and disappointed. He desperately wanted to hear his father say the magic words and now he would never hear them. There would always be the unfilled vacuum because his father couldn't tell him that he loved him.

Children who live in ambivalence are miserable. They want to believe that their parents love them but they can't be sure. Like working a puzzle, they are left to put the pieces together the best they can. But like many old puzzles, some of the pieces are missing and the total picture will be impossible to complete.

Silence is painful because we are left to interpret the missing words. We all know how hard it can be to understand what is said; trying to decipher what is not said is maddening.

I am astonished at people who say they read something "between the lines." Where do we learn to read what isn't written? Most of us aren't as good at "filling in the gaps" as we like to think.

Recently an actress was being interviewed about her famous father. The host asked her, "But you do believe your father loved you, don't you?"

Her reply was, "Yes, I really think he did."

The answer seemed hopeful, even positive, but there was no tone of confidence in her voice or expression of pleasure in her face. She spoke wistfully.

Children without this confidence spend their lives trying to build a case that their parents loved them. They exaggerate their parents' signs of affection; they dig deeply to excavate any clues that may support love; they rationalize their parents' continued absences.

It is as though they are in a court of law arguing the fact that they are real human beings. They need *prima facie* evidence that their parents did in fact love them. Carefully they arrange all the data, hoping that their argument to themselves is finally convincing.

Words are not enough, but neither are actions. We are only finally persuaded when we have seen both. When someone tells us they love us in an attempt to manipulate our behavior, we quickly learn how hollow the expression is. On the other hand, toys and electronics cannot substitute the magically reassuring terms of endearment.

Some Children Never Doubt Our Love for Them

Not every child swims hopelessly at sea mulling over the question of parental love. It is not true that children are inevitably confused. Even teenagers in the midst of great rebellion, frustration, and anger can still know that their parents love them. Prolonged doubt about parental love is neither necessary nor inevitable.

Occasionally we hear someone describe their childhood in these terms: "We were poor but there was so much love we didn't even notice it." Their facial expression, tone of voice, and the sparkle in their eyes tell you how much they mean it. The presence of genuine love can rise above all the obstacles and heartaches that families may have to confront.

These children have experienced a love not attached to things. If we convey love by giving tangible objects, we must continue to give these things or belief in our love will collapse when the gifts stop. On the other hand, love that expresses itself in caring, listening, availability, and sacrifice can be seen for its own value and retained in the hearts of our children long after they leave home.

How Do They Feel?

Books and seminars can't adequately tell us how our children feel. We have to ask them and listen well if we want to know what is going on inside.

When our children were very young we moved to a house south of Sterling, Kansas. Running in front of our country home was a paved road. Cars flew by without touching their brakes.

Soon after we arrived, I took the children out to the road and explained how dangerous it was. They were never to go onto the road, and they never did.

Before long Jim acquired a small dog, a mutt we called Ginger. Ginger enjoyed roaming out onto the highway and chasing cars. Unfortunately, Ginger never excelled at racing cars and one day he got hit.

The dog was killed instantly, and as it lay motionless on the road, our four-year-old son came out of the house. I knew how traumatic this first brush with death could be in Jim's young life. I had to handle it correctly and sensitively. If I messed up, Jim could grow up with a quirk or a twitch and any number of psychological problems (I thought).

I tried to comfort him, and said compassionately, in my best parental tone, "Don't worry, Jim; we're going to bury Ginger." I got the old car out of the garage, and with a shovel carefully put Ginger's body in the trunk, and Jim and I drove to the site.

I dug a hole and carefully placed Ginger in it. Unfortunately, the little grave was too small. I said to myself, *Be cool. You don't want Jim to get any emotional scars from this.*

"Don't worry, Jim," I repeated. "We'll just dig a larger hole."

Jim looked up at me and said simply, "Why don't you just chop his legs off?"

Today Jim is fine, but I have a quirk and a twitch.

We can never be certain how our children really feel unless we talk to them, ask questions, and come to an understanding with each other. To simply shrug and say we know how the other must feel is to trample over the people we love, and not show a personal interest in their unique personality.

The special relationship that God the Father and God the Son enjoy is one where feelings are vocalized. With Peter, James, and John as witnesses, God said, "This is my Son, whom I love; with him I am well pleased. Listen to him!" (Matt. 17:5)

God the Father expressed His feelings for His Son

openly on many occasions (Matt. 3:17; 12:18). Likewise, Christ was comfortable voicing His love for people and teaching the importance of expressing our love for each other (John 13:34).

Recently, Pat and I received a note from one of our grown children that began with the words "I love you because . . ." The greeting-card people don't print anything as effective and heartwarming as that piece of paper and its caring message.

Most of us have at one time had some difficulty expressing our love. Sometimes families fear the expression has sexual connotations and wonder how it will be received.

One of our children said to us one time, "I don't know why I can't tell my parents I love them." It's awkward, especially through the adolescent years when children are struggling so hard with their identities. But if children are to become comfortable with the expression of love and its meaning, they need to have good role modeling. It will take a Herculean effort for a young adult to say "I love you" to a parent who has never said it to the child.

Children seem to begin life with a strong concept of parental love. The young children I have talked to about the subject seem confident that their mothers and fathers love them. The teenage years seem to be the time when the estrangement begins. Maybe it's because many parents have and express mixed emotions, and often aren't sure if they *do* love this exploding adolescent.

The challenge is to keep expressing love to a teenager who doesn't want to hear it. Parents who can verbalize it under those conditions have something close to a God-like love.

When he was a teenager, Gary tried his best to drive his parents nuts. He broke curfews, took the car without permission, became impossible to live with, and flatly challenged his parents by saying, "Why don't you throw me out? Go ahead, throw me out."

Gary's parents remained steady through all of the abuse, even when they thought they couldn't take any more. They consistently reassured their son that they loved him even when they felt like imbeciles saying it. Eventually Gary's hostility abated, and as he matured Gary learned to tell his parents that he loved them, too.

These people remained models when it was tough to care. Later they reaped the rewards of holding steady when it would have been easy to give up.

No one knows what the Holy Spirit will accomplish in young lives. But parents need to supply as much seed as possible for the Spirit of God to cultivate.

Dating Your Children

Early in our family experience I read about how important it was to "date" your children, and I was willing to take someone else's advice.

I'll never forget the excitement on Mary's face when I asked her, as a five-year-old, if she would go out for dinner all alone with her father.

"Yes, yes," Mary said, her voice racing, her body almost dancing in place. "I have to get my shoes," she explained. Then, pointing her finger at me she said, "I'll be right back."

Mary disappeared into her room for a second and then reappeared. "Don't go away," she reminded me.

The look on her face said she was so overjoyed to go out with her father that she didn't want to miss it for anything.

Love, to be real, must be translated into action. Love has to be spoken, and demonstrated, if it is to be perceived as fact. Children don't understand the theories of love. Neither do they grasp subtle love that lurks in the background like shadows at dusk. Children can easily interpret up-front, direct acts of caring love and attention.

Dating our children is one of the great memory builders. It creates a feeling of security, attachment, and personal worth in them that few other events can do with as much success.

A parent's affection cannot cure all of a child's problems. But without enough evidence of parental love, life becomes severely difficult for them. Ask any adult who was deprived of parental love. That deprivation leaves a wound that may never be completely healed. They spend their old age wondering if their parents loved them or secretly rejected them.

The children who see and feel the love of their parents usually find it easier to comprehend the love of God. If we can't relate to the idea of parental love, we may misunderstand the image of a Heavenly Father who loves us. The apostle Paul draws on the analogy of motherly love when he tells us:

> As apostles of Christ we could have been a burden to you, but we were gentle among you, like a mother caring for her little children. We loved you so much that we were delighted to share with you not only the gospel of God but our lives as well, because you had become so dear to us. (1 Thess. 2:7-8)

Angry Love Is Hard to Recognize

Many parents love their children very much but find themselves angry at them most of the time. Their problem may be that they _feel_ love but don't have the foggiest concept of how to express it. And they may secretly fear losing their children.

The angry-love type holds a tight leash on the child and constantly shouts disapproval. It isn't that the parent doesn't care. They may care very much. But because they communicate it in such a negative way they create a serious dilemma in the child.

The child begins to perceive love and anger as synonymous. He or she will learn to dislike love or avoid its expression because love is overbearing, binding, and hurtful.

Occasional anger directed at outright disobedience or disrespect can be quite healthy in a love relationship. If it is expressed honestly and clearly, anger can even reinforce love. But continuous, unabated anger that is sporadic and irrational buries love, making it unrecognizable.

When a father demonstrates one constant emotion—anger—the child has little chance of detecting and identifying the father's love for him or her. Because many men are only comfortable in their role as father while expressing anger, millions of children know nothing of fatherly love.

Love is a poor alloy. If we mix love and meanness, only the taste of meanness lingers. If we mix love and legalism, our children will taste the bitterness of legalism. Mix love and selfishness and our children smell only the stench of selfishness. Combine love and insecurity and like cream the insecurity will rise to the top.

Pure love is hard to find, but love must be the predominant ingredient. Children soon recognize when they are being used. They can filter out the difference between true love and ulterior motives, and when they do, they come to resent the foul mix.

As soon as possible we must love our children for their best interest and not for our own. Only then will we communicate real love.

When Mary was only seven years old I was forced

to ask myself if I had the courage to show her pure love. Mary asked if she could attend a harmless Disney movie with a group of friends. Immediately I wondered what people might say at the church where I pastored. Was a movie too controversial? Finally I told Mary, "Of course you can go." The church was not going to raise my child. I had to deal with her request openly, honestly, and not play foolish mind games. The loving thing to do was whatever was good for Mary. God expects that much of us as parents.

Thanks for...

Forgetting What We Said

Late in the evening, Melanie and her mother were having a heated argument. As a teenager, Melanie didn't think she needed a curfew. But her grades were slumping badly, and her mother was barking again about how messy her daughter's bedroom was.

Suddenly Melanie stood up, pulled at her hair and screamed, "I hate living here! I hate everything about it."

They weren't the first mother and daughter to exchange angry accusations after a serious disagreement. And like most people would, they each took it personally. Both mother and daughter displayed their rage and hurt the other—at least enough to get the other's attention.

Words spoken rashly in the heat of argument present problems. We tend to take them personally, and then hold on to them for a long time. It's true that words can't physically hurt us, but we sometimes take words and press them into our own hearts like a dagger.

At the age of twenty-one, Melanie dropped out of technical school and asked her mother if she could come back home to live for a while.

Can you imagine what her mother said? "I thought you hated living here!" After five years, she picked up the conversation as if it had taken place that morning. The concept was fresh and the words still hurt. While Melanie's mother didn't rehearse the scene every day, she had reminded herself of it enough to keep it alive.

Because they had never openly discussed the feelings that caused the original outburst, the mother assumed the feelings were still there and unchanged. Who knows how many unfinished conversations were still rattling around in both of their minds?

Unfinished Conversations

How many unresolved confrontations do we carry around with us? Could you write down half a dozen painful and puzzling conversations you have had with your children and never gotten to the bottom of? Lying just beneath the surface of our conscious minds like resting crocodiles, they may be ready to snap at the most unexpected moment.

Did you ever hear anything like:

> I never get anything. You always loved Wendy more than me. When I get out of this house I'm never coming back. I know I'll treat my kids a lot better than this. I can't do anything around here.

A father had an ugly confrontation with his daughter and they were no longer speaking. Soon afterward, while poking around her room, he found a terse note that said simply, "I hate Dad."

He tried to handle the message philosophically, but it wasn't easy. Reassuring himself that she didn't mean it, he pushed the message to the back of his brain and suppressed it. But during the next few years, whenever he and his daughter had a serious run-in, those words would reappear on his memory screen.

Fortunately, he finally came to see the statement as a normal display of adolescent anger. And though he and his daughter are now close, that father had to consciously, deliberately put the incident into its proper perspective.

Knowing the human condition, God teaches us in His Word to use healing words when we are insulted. We only exacerbate the situation by saying hurtful things in return.

"Reckless words pierce like a sword, but the tongue of the wise brings healing" (Prov. 12:18).

Did They Mean What They Said?

When children or teenagers say something cruel or hurtful to their parents, do they mean it as harshly as it sounds? That's the nagging question. Usually someone hurls an insult and then one of two things happens: The other person shoots an insult back, or the perpetrator walks off in a huff. The intention was to hurt and not to heal. And because the problem usually isn't examined at the time, we are left to speculate on how seriously the words were meant.

So let's speculate! The young person probably meant what he or she said *at the time.* When they said *hate,* they probably meant *hate.* In that particular context, at that particular time, he or she expressed the feelings churning inside. When your son says he hates his brother or sister, at that particular time he does feel hate for his brother or sister.

But loving parents immediately defend their children. They agree that Johnny and Jeannie were under a lot of pressure; they weren't eating properly; they don't know the meaning of the word; or they have been watching too much television.

Rationalize if you choose, but most likely when teenagers say they hate living in that house, they mean that right now they hate living in that house. At the moment your daughter says she hates her brother, don't tell her she doesn't.

Seldom does a child or a teenager have trouble with vocabulary at the primitive level. They know what hate, jealousy, anger, frustration, and disappointment mean. Most likely they meant exactly what they said when they said it.

What we lose by not discussing the situation at the time or as soon as possible afterward is not finding out *why* they felt the way they did. We fail to get to the bottom of it. Because of our inability or lack of opportunity to deal with it at the time, we remain befuddled by the confrontation.

Release May Come

Under the best of circumstances our children may someday free us from those haunting memories. If they do, the release is a miracle of the first magnitude. In my case two of our young adult children wiped the slate clean, each with one broad swipe.

It is incredible how much a brief statement can affect our lives. When my son Jim was in his early twenties, he and I were in some discussion. I have no idea how the conversation began, but almost childishly I said to Jim, "Yeah, but you didn't care too much for your father when you were young."

"Oh, that was nothing," Jim explained. "Teenagers aren't supposed to like their fathers; that has nothing to do with today."

That was the statement I had waited years to hear. Always suspicious that Jim deeply resented me, I struggled to define our relationship in terms I could enjoy. But I always recalled his clear indications that he thought I was about as useful as sock lint.

Because Jim released me from that burden of separation, I was free to forget the pain of the past. Not that I can't remember some of the things he said, but they don't hurt anymore. They are no longer real to me.

In order to be free, I don't have to say he didn't mean what he said. The important element is that he doesn't mean it now. I am free to accept Jim and his assessment of me today. I don't have to haul yesterday around like a broken wagon.

Forgiving and forgetting are like a nut and its shell. They are closely related and both are necessary if they are to bring fruit to maturity. The rudeness and insults of yesterday have to be cast off if we are to enjoy today's sweet fruit.

Our daughter Mary supplied another releasing statement. We were in a hot discussion over the phone when I indelicately reminded her of what she had said years earlier: "You used to say that you hated family deals like that," I jabbed her.

"Oh, that's just one of those things, isn't it?" Mary countered. "That was something I said as a teenager. Look, Dad, why don't you just erase everything I said in high school and let's start all over again."

That one sentence was powerful enough to cut the chains. Some words, statements, and even actions I have never forgotten. I rehash them, memorizing them better than I ever did Bible verses. But Mary punched in *erase* on my memory disk. Those painful words are removed from the tape if I will allow them to be. I could search for them again if I choose, but how pointless and destructive if she no longer means them.

If I can forget what she said in high school, she can certainly forget some of the things I said to her. In the heated, changing turmoil of being a parent, we likewise say irresponsible things. We also need to tell our children that those misspent statements mean nothing today.

What Does It Mean to Forget?

If you have had surgery in the past, you are not likely to forget it. But you probably don't still suffer from pre-surgery anxiety or post-surgery pain. We can perhaps remember the pain, but we can't *feel* the pain anymore.

Maybe you can remember your teenager calling you a nerd. But forgetting the incident means you no longer feel the sting. On the other hand, if you can recall it "just like it was yesterday," the feelings are still close to the surface.

If we fail to reduce the sharpness of the memory, we are destined to collapse into bitterness. Bitterness will prevent us from ever having an open, trusting relationship with our children.

Yesterday, I saw a woman on television who said that she was conceived as a result of rape. As a young adult she found her father and forgave him for the terrible act of raping the woman who was her mother. She explained that the Lord had been good to her and she could not withhold forgiveness from someone who had made a mistake—no matter how horrendous that mistake had been.

How and when a person forgives and forgets is a personal choice. Each of us must wrestle with God over the decision. As a pure and generous act of love, our ability to forget opens great opportunities for fresh and new relationships. Many Christians have been able to forgive terrible deeds and abusive comments, and then erase the board clean. If they stared hard enough at the board they could make out the dim markings of the past, but the beauty of the Christian life is that we can refuse to search the board for the old traces.

When we not only forgive, but forget, we no longer hold any bitterness toward those who have offended us by word or action.

Clean the Slate

Every parent and grown child should consider wiping the slate clean. We probably can't remember every insulting or mean thing we said while living through the difficult years of adolescence. That can be good and bad. Our children may remember some things we fail to recall.

Because the adolescent years are muddled, every parent would be wise to make a sweeping but sincere statement of contrition and absolution. Tell the young person or persons in your life to forget every harmful, hateful thing you said during those turbulent years. Then assure them that you will also forget the offensive things they may have said.

You aren't starting over completely. You can't really do that. And there are good times and good things said that we shouldn't forget. Simply promise to pull out the arrows and let the wounds heal.

If I Could Raise My Children Again

The following is not a list of regrets, but rather ways I would fine-tune my family relationships if I had it to do over again. (They are not listed in order of importance.)

1. I would make Sunday afternoons more interesting and take fewer naps.
2. I would find hobbies to share with each of my children.
3. I would be a patient listener instead of a hurry-up listener.
4. I would never spend a chilly night in a dismal airport chasing a career on my daughter's birthday.
5. I would pray more with my children.
6. I would let my children teach me.
7. I would go camping with my son twice as much as I did.

8. I would date their mother more.
9. I would celebrate their victories more.
10. I would give them an extended family.
11. I would carry my son around on my shoulders more often and tell him that I love him.
12. I would keep my sense of humor while they were going through puberty.
13. I would never discipline them over grades.
14. I would stop arguing about their messy rooms after the age of thirteen and save my energy for more important things.
15. I would chill out more.
16. I would involve the family in more projects in which we could help others.

But the opportunities for all this are gone. Better yet, I think I'll love them for today and express it whenever possible.

Keeping
Your Hands
in Your
Pockets

When Gary reached his fortieth birthday, he told his wife Maria that he had no idea how much his parents must have sacrificed and worried while he was growing up. It had never dawned on him—not until he had two teenagers of his own did he begin to realize how much money it takes to support a family.

Children don't have a clue how difficult it can be to earn money. Neither do teenagers, or young adults, for that matter. They can't understand what it takes to buy shoes for five people until they are responsible for a family of five. Unable to appreciate income and outgo, they tend to think parents have more money than they let on.

While they don't really believe money grows on trees, they are suspicious that it can be found on a few select bushes. As any parent knows, children lack realism.

Recently, I sat with a group of college students as they contemplated how much money they expected to earn after graduation. They tossed some figures around and wondered how they could ever spend that much money. Little did they know that the figures they were talking about would never be enough to support a family in the style they dreamed of. And I didn't have the heart to tell them.

Money and Affection

Understandably, children have an inadequate concept of money. They can't grasp the full picture. Consequently, parents are foolish to try to impress their children by spending money on them. We can't buy enough cars, household conveniences, or clothes to dazzle our children. They believe in easy-come, easy-go and are willing to spend all the money their parents can possibly dig up.

This is why it doesn't work to try to buy their affection. Children don't see materialism as a sign of affection. They see it as something a parent owes them. They also see money as something the parent has little difficulty acquiring.

The parent who believes he can gain closeness with a child by providing more *things* is speeding down the highway of disappointment to a tragic end. We can demonstrate affection by giving them our time, attention, and availability, but cash will never cause our children to ultimately believe we love them. Some parents are aware of this and throw money at their children anyway. They assume that because they can't be around their children all the time, they might as well give them cash.

It feels great to provide good things for our children. Indeed the Bible teaches that we should be good providers (1 Tim. 5:8). But we should also remind ourselves what money will *not* buy.

Money will not buy love.
Money will not buy gratitude.
Money will not provide experience.
Money will not substitute time and attention.

Many parents will attempt to use money to accomplish these things anyway. Go ahead and try, but it won't work!

They Think We Owe It to Them

For some strange, inexplicable reason, children generally have the attitude that parents owe them everything that is available. They believe that what they see on television: the toys, the fancy cereals, the houses, the boats, the cars—whatever is so graphically presented to their young eyes—is theirs for the asking.

To a point, they are right. As parents, we owe them the basics of life, and a child's natural faith believes the parent can provide those things. Food, clothing, and housing are fundamental necessities. If possible, we owe them good food, decent clothing, and proper housing. If a child needs tennis shoes, he or she shouldn't be the only child at school without them—if they can possibly be provided.

The plea of Proverbs applies to children as well: "Keep falsehood and lies from me; give me neither poverty nor riches, but give me only my daily bread" (30:8).

Parents may be poor and the children suffer from too little. This is unfortunate, but on the other side of the coin, if we have enough, we need to control how much is too much for our children.

Our need for acceptance and approval from our children forces us to make irrational decisions. There is a happy middle and it is probably closer to the lower half than we might think.

A seasoned school counselor who raised a family of his own said, "If I had it to do over again, I would give my children less, not more." But when you are involved in raising the child, those decisions are tough to make.

One of our biggest lessons came when our son Jim was nominated for Homecoming king. It's a big event at any school, and Jim told us he would need a suit for the crowning ceremony. Conscientious parents that we were, we took him shopping and he picked out a beautiful dark blue suit complete with a vest. The cost was $200.00 (a king's ransom at the time), but it looked great on the guy.

Finally the big night came, and Jim left the house in his new threads. We were pleased at how happy he was, and started to get ourselves ready for the ceremony. Within minutes, Jim came running back into the house and disappeared into his room. Soon he bolted out again, wearing pants and a sweater. "The guys decided against suits!" he shouted as he fled out the door, leaving us bewildered—and broke.

Easy-come, easy-go. After all, it's only money.

The Pressure Could Kill You

If you try to buy everything your children can imagine, plus half the things you dream up yourselves, it's easy to crumble under the pressure.

Interestingly, parents tend to buy for their children and neglect their own needs. Later, when the children reach about forty, they wonder how and why their parents did it. In many cases, they wish their parents hadn't done so much for them, and that they had taken better care of themselves—taken some trips, put something away for retirement, dressed in better clothes.

Parents are spending more and more time away from home earning money so they can buy more things for their children—as if that will prove how much they love their children. The truth is, children would rather have their parents around more, even if it means less *things*. But parents seem determined to give them more things and less of themselves.

The old adages are true. Buy an expensive toy and watch the child play with the box. Take your children to California and watch them play in the sand as they do in their own backyard.

Years ago, we took the entire family to the East Coast for a month of vacation. We visited the United States Capitol, stayed in a cabin on the Chesapeake Bay, swam in the ocean, went boating, caught crabs. The Super Family packed in as much activity as possible.

When we arrived home, I asked the children to take a few minutes to write down what they liked most about the trip. Their number-one answer was the traffic jams. They enjoying inching along for hours, watching the beads of perspiration form on the back of Daddy's neck. They were mesmerized with the bumper-to-bumper experience, while cars overheated and tempers flared.

Next summer, instead of Six Flags or Disney World, why not take your family around Chicago for a couple of hours during rush-hour traffic? Who knows, maybe they'll think you're their hero.

What I'm saying is this: Slow down. Cut yourself some slack. Aim at personal attention rather than killing yourself in order to supply the wrong things.

A college student wrote to her parents and warned them against helping too much. She realized that her financial situation was tough sometimes, but she felt that was probably the best way for her to learn responsibility. If her parents kept "bailing her out," she would take that much longer learning to make it on her own.

Not many parents get notes like that, but if we're honest we know the principle is true. If we take all our childrens' financial pressures on ourselves, we are likely to cause two injuries. First, we deny our children the opportunity to learn responsibility. Second, we assume more pressure than we can or should handle.

The lessons of warding off scarcity and poverty have to be learned by all of us. If our children learn to work hard and pay their way, they can face financial setback and still survive by the grace of God. By dumping money on our children we only stall the lessons that Proverbs would teach us:

> A little sleep, a little slumber, a little folding of the hands to rest—and poverty will come on you like a bandit and scarcity like an armed man (6:10, 11).

Buying the Big House

Nearly ten years ago we got a few extra dollars and decided to purchase a better home. It's a two-story brick house on a double lot. We live in Nebraska, but because I grew up in Washington, D.C., the Eastern design of the house especially appealed to me.

I felt like Super Dad moving my family from the old frame house to this spacious-but-not-outlandish home. The children were certain to be excited. It seemed like the typical mid-American move, and I knew my family would adore me for it.

After all, everyone got their own bedroom; we have a good-sized family room, lots of bathrooms and closet space. At the old house, June lived in a tiny sewing room, and we all shared one bathroom, without a shower.

However, from day one, it became obvious that the dream was mine and it never really became theirs. Not that they were ungrateful, it was just that they liked the old house, complete with all its flaws and inconveniences.

For the past decade, my life has been controlled by a substantial home mortgage and all the bills that accompany it. Recently, I asked the children if they would be disappointed if we sold the house. No problem to them; they weren't attached to it anyway.

As our children have launched into their twenties, they have become more expressive than ever and have thanked us for many things. But no one has ever thanked us for the house. Nothing wrong with that— they simply never were fond of buildings.

There is something reaffirming about that. It makes me dare to hope that we will always care for one another as individuals. The kind of house they own or car they drive will never mean anything in particular to me. And it seems material things don't mean a great deal to them. I know I won't have to buy a submarine or a blimp to keep their attention. We will be able to enjoy one another for many years to come on a personal level.

Poor but Wise

Do you have a list of values—what you would like your children to become? If you do, the list probably consists of some of the following:

Good-natured

Caring
Wise
Contented
Educated
Christ-centered
Health-conscious
Loving
Creative
Confident
Friendly

Add to the list as many qualities as you like. Then arrange them in order of priority. Which are the most important to you? Begin to work toward instilling in your children the most significant qualities—values that will last them a lifetime. Someday they will thank you for it.

"Better a poor but wise youth than an old but foolish king who no longer knows how to take warning" (Eccles. 4:13).

Doing without is something every young person should experience occasionally. Someone has said, "The wealthy never have the thrill of making that final payment."

While no one exactly thanks their parents for bouts with poverty, many young adults will admit what a great school it was. They learned to appreciate sacrifice, patience, delayed gratification, and hard work. Some children rebel against its lessons and later become foolish spenders, always living on the edge of financial disaster. We can't control those decisions. But at least we can expose our children to measured spending.

No one knows if he can live on a meager income until he gives it a try. Children need to learn that it is possible to survive under dire circumstances.

The apostle Paul apparently lived with and without sufficient income: "I know what it is to be in need, and I know what it is to have plenty. I have learned the secret of being content in any and every situation, whether well fed or hungry, whether living in plenty or in want. I can do everything through him who gives me strength'' (Phil. 4:12, 13).

How unfortunate if our children learn only the lessons of plenty.

It's
Your
Life

When our children are quite young, we imagine that we can deliver a perfect package. We will raise our children thus and so and they will "turn out" exactly as we planned. Countless books and tapes, as well as numerous seminars and radio programs, tell us how to produce the desired type of child.

If we want a pure child, for instance, there are certain do's and don'ts for his upbringing. If we want a believing child, we add other qualities. If we want our child to be athletic, we'll need to buy a special ball. If intelligence is the most important quality to us, we buy a set of books. The air is full these days of parental guidelines. By supplying the correct ingredients we imagine that we can produce whatever kind of child we want.

What is not taught enough is how to let go of our children so that they can be (1) whatever God wants them to be, and (2) whatever they choose to become. The need to control our children's destinies is harmful and divisive. Few adult children will ever thank us for controlling their lives.

Many parents have trouble extending this kind of personal freedom. They can't bring themselves to give their teenager the keys to life. There is a fear that their child will open the wrong doors and go in bizarre directions.

That fear is real and mistakes are possible, but eventually the reins to life have to be handed over. Young people cannot simply live out their parents' expectations.

We Can't Relive Our Lives

It's hard to believe some of the dumb things I've said to our children. Our daughter, Mary, has excellent skills in English, so naturally I spelled out her life for her one day.

"Now, what you want to do, Mary, is to go after your strengths. Get a Ph.D. in English. Then you can settle down in a small college and teach. On the side you will have time to write."

Instantly, without emotion, Mary replied, "That's what you wish you had done, isn't it?"

I was caught. I had been telling her it was *her* life, and at the same time I was telling her what to do with it—sure that I knew what she would enjoy. I wanted to pick up my child and transfer her into the perfect world I had envisioned.

That's what overly protective parents do. It can be done covertly or overtly, but the idea is to move them into the fantasy world we picture. Whether it's football or cheerleading or ministry or a business career, we want our lives to extend into theirs—even though we protest that we aren't really doing that.

Every once in a while we get caught. We may shroud it in terms like: "All we really want for you is what the Lord wants for you." And then we begin adjusting their lives to match our expectations.

Raise Your Children to Release Them

There are some things we can't hold on to. We can't capture rainbows. They can't be trapped and put into jars. We can't reduce them to wallet-size and carry them around with us. Rainbows arc across the sky with their own beauty and freedom. We enjoy them while they're there, but we can't keep them with us forever.

Anyone who raises children in order to keep them doesn't understand rainbows, birds, songs—or people. The imprisoned child is miserable, tormented, thwarted. If we try to control our children, we are simply responding to our own insecurities and fears.

God doesn't shove people into cages, nor does He attempt to fit them into molds. Neither does He expect parents to box their children in and hold them captive to their own private dreams.

In the play *Marty*, the mother is emotionally dependent on her grown son. When he meets a special girl and begins to care for her very much, he naturally spends less and less time with his mother.

When the frightened, insecure parent figures out what is going on, she raises objections. Her son's happiness is running contrary to hers. Desperate, the mother works hard to separate the two young people and keep her son for herself.

Not many of us are that brazen, but neither are we total strangers to the idea. The release of our children to the embrace of another is frequently a hard pill to swallow.

The leave and cleave principle is one of God's earliest references to relationships. He tells us that a man must leave his parents and cleave to his wife (Gen. 2:24).

In some cases, after young people have been out on their own, they may need to return home for a while, but the principle remains. Don't give them the freedom to leave and then force them to remain dependent upon you. Children have the need and the right to be released from the nest to fly on their own.

The Support Remains

At a recent family seminar one of the young participants explained what he appreciated about his parents: "They've always been supportive. If I want to become a lawyer, or an insurance agent, or whatever, they're all for me. I've never felt they were trying to manipulate me in any direction."

The smile on his face and the pride in his voice were moving. I had the feeling he wouldn't be afraid to go home and tell his parents that he had decided to run a hot dog stand in Boa Boa.

Not every parent feels that supportive of whatever their child may choose to do with his or her life. Many are deeply into goal-setting for their young people, and many reap a whirlwind because of it.

"It's your life" has to be said sincerely and often. Our children claim that Pat and I said it a million times. We only admit to half a million. Either way, we got the message across.

They are hard words to say—and mean. A number of times our children tested what we thought were appalling career and job choices. It was difficult not to speak up. If asked, we said how we felt or at least hinted at it. On rare occasions we said something devious like, "Well, Lynn tried that; maybe you'll want to talk to her."

When Mary enrolled in law school, we wondered

if she had weighed the consequences, but we were very happy for her. When Jim took a job tearing out asbestos, we nearly went apoplectic, but we managed to joke with him about the dangers. When June decided to teach music, we told her she would be great at it.

Our children know more about who they are and where they fit in than we do. They also have the right and privilege to make their own choices—and mistakes. And the real benefit is that they have the opportunity to chase their own joys.

When a child becomes a young adult, accountability shifts away from the parents to the individual and their own relationship to God. If they have peace working in a car wash, who are we to say they should have been an astronaut? It's an act of faith to release our young people and emotionally support their life choices.

Our support is perhaps most important on the emotional level. The parent who withholds emotional support or fights the child's decision hangs a millstone around that young person's neck. Young people don't necessarily need their parents' money; they don't need their parents to pull strings; and they may not want advice. But they do need a warm hug, an encouraging smile, and any other signal of genuine acceptance.

The Bible tells us, "So then, each of us will give an account of himself to God" (Rom. 14:12).

We should be content with that. Young persons old enough to be out on their own don't have to give an account of their life to their parents. God loves them, and will guide them in their choices.

Following in Our Footsteps

Often parents desire their children to follow in their footsteps simply because the parent has personal needs. As we grow old, we want our children to validate our existence. We are in essence asking their stamp of approval on who we are and what we've done with our lives. Because of our own insecurities, we sometimes look to our adolescent children, hoping they will confirm that our life has meaning.

The following are some of the things we mistakenly ask our children to do or be primarily to justify ourselves as their parents:

Be Intelligent. Most of us realize that we could have done better in school, and we hope our children will excel partly to prove that point. We say we push them for their own benefit, but sometimes that statement is a mask to cover up the need to validate ourselves. Setting up a child to fulfill our dreams is extremely dangerous.

Be Athletic. It's fun to watch a child get a hit in Little League, or to see him go out for football, but it becomes distorted if we see that hit as the one we failed to get in our youth, or making it first-string on the football team as a consolation because we didn't make it.

Be Accepted. Instead of letting our children find their own social niche, we try to create one for them. We want them to be popular, well-liked, because we would like to have been there. We may anxiously hurry them into dating situations because we remember how painful it was for us to wait and wonder if we'd ever have a date.

Be a Believer. In a frenzied struggle we want them to match or exceed our Christian experience rather than find their own at their own pace. Afraid of what others in the church might think, we are tempted to rush them into honorable activities so our family will appear spiritual. We sometimes worry that their walk with Christ will be odd or unusual, a shade different from our own.

Each parent can assemble his or her own list of *Be's*. We all have varied expectations, and our children react to each of them differently. One young person in a household complies while another in the same house rebels. We may have trouble deciding what is in the best interest of our teenager and what is merely a personal need or wish of our own. Smart parents will try to avoid self-serving expectations.

I know a man who is the head of a prosperous business. He built it up from scratch, and made almost all his dreams of success come true. The culminating factor would be that his son someday step in and take over the business. To the man's chagrin, his son wants to become a beachcomber in California.

But this father set the stage in his own mind—it was entirely his dream. Despite his otherwise successful life, the father created a built-in guaranteed failure. He didn't count on his son having a mind of his own.

That story can be multiplied on the plains of Nebraska, the streets of Los Angeles, or the back-country of Alaska. We weave a web to trap our own children and then we are terribly disappointed if they escape.

All of us have unfinished business—mountains we have not climbed, commitments we have not kept, weight we have not lost, cities we have not visited, hungry people we have not fed. Be careful that your unfinished business isn't dumped on your children with the unreasonable expectation that they complete it for you.

Our concept of personal freedom is greatly affected by our theology. If we believe that God controls our every thought and movement, it's easier to think we should have control over our children. On the other hand, if we believe God gives us a wide range of choice and flexibility, we can offer the same freedom to our teenagers. They will make mistakes, just as we have made them, but God has graciously given us all that option.

Going to My Games—but Not All of Them

Organized sports are really more than a game. Winning is all-important to many coaches and managers, and when it's equally important to parents, many young people get crushed under the pressure. Most of us suffer from the embarrassment of not having excelled in sports. Many young people suffer the pain of not getting into a game, or of having been selected late for a team.

Grateful is the child whose parents refused to take sports too seriously. He or she can be eternally thankful that their parents saw athletics as a game, not a measure of individual importance.

Grateful too are those whose dads didn't *compete* with them but simply played the game with them. They didn't attempt to endorse their manhood by beating their child in a game of sports.

Grateful is the son or daughter who was not

117

pushed into sports when he or she did not care to participate. Their parent did not attempt to be the phantom coach driving their child to victory.

Grateful are the young people whose parents didn't try to live out their athletic dreams through their children, trying to make them into the sports stars they never were.

Young people usually appreciate attention; it helps build good self-esteem. What is important is the correct dose given at the right time. Too much attention at the wrong time tends to make a child self-centered. They can begin to believe the world should stop and watch them perform.

It takes a skilled parent to know when to pour on the attention and when to hold back. Parents must learn when to make a "big deal" out of something and when to let it slide.

The Family Circle

The following diagrams show three types of family circles. Each type has its strengths and weaknesses.

Parent-centered

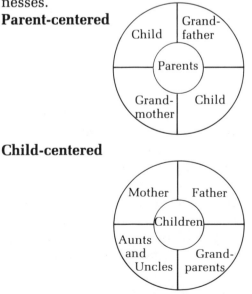

Child-centered

Family-centered

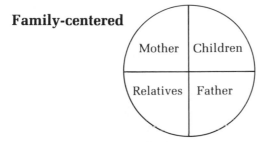

The problem with the parent-centered family circle is that the desires and ambitions of the parents are *the* major consideration. Children and extended family members are made to feel unimportant; their opinions, feelings and desires are ignored.

The child-centered circle makes the child the center of everything. Every event stops and every calendar schedule is rewritten to make way for whatever activity the child is involved in. The parents are reluctant to allow their children to benefit from some activity that does not revolve around them.

The family-centered circle says everyone is important. It teaches equal value and respect for each member of the extended family. Everyone is special, but no one is more special than anyone else. That is the only acceptable way to understand "special" in a family context. Special means equal as well as unique.

Saturday Morning Sports

Trying to keep the family-centered circle balanced isn't always easy. It's difficult to give a young person plenty of attention without too much attention.

When June was in junior high school, she joined an intramural basketball team. Each Saturday morning the blue team played the yellow team or vice versa. I didn't attend every game, just as I didn't go to every Little League game in the summer.

One Friday night June pressed me hard to get up and go to her basketball game the next morning. I explained to her how I thought parents should stay away once in a while and just let the kids play without the pressure of parents in the stands. Oh, but she needed me there, she said. After all, "all of the parents" come to the Saturday morning intramurals.

Finally I caved in. Early the next day I dragged my weary body to the old gymnasium at Aurora High School and up the bleacher steps. Settling myself down at mid-court, I looked around for other parents. There were none. I was the only parent in attendance that day.

The whistle blew and June came running onto the court. I'll never forget the huge grin on her face as she looked up and spotted me in the bleachers. Beaming, she dribbled down the court with one hand while she looked up at the solitary parent, clapping his hands and chanting, "Go, June!"

I'm glad I went to that game. At that particular point in time it was important to June that I be there. And kids have to know they're important. Just don't allow them to get to the place where the world must come to a screeching halt because there's a game on. There are other events in families that are of equal importance and must be considered. I salute the parent who finds the balance.

The Big Leagues

Like most parents, I can remember our children giving it their all in sports—Jim as a first-rate outfielder and excellent cross-country runner, Mary racing around the circle at an AWANA rally, and June playing basketball her junior year of high school.

It was at a girls' basketball game that I watched

sports go crazy. As the game progressed, some of the parents began to complain loudly at the officials. Forty- and fifty-year-old parents grew increasingly obnoxious and eventually vulgar.

After a heated exchange, a teenaged boy sitting in the bleachers told a parent to sit down and shut up. In turn the parent invited the boy outside to settle.

That's the big leagues—grown adults involved in their children's games to the point of absurdity. The game ceased to be a game. They turned it into war. They made a high school sports event the most important activity of the week.

There are other ways to let our children know how much we love and appreciate them without putting them on a pedestal. If we make them out to be a hero because they scored a goal in a football game, we are in essence saying that is one of the most important accomplishments of their lives. Sports must be kept in proper perspective to other successes.

Teenagers will eventually be thankful for parents who enjoyed their games without putting the pressure on to excel.

One dad drove his son to basketball practice every Saturday morning. An ex-jock himself, this father worked hard to mold his son into a fine-tuned athlete.

After losing an intramural game, the father spoke sternly to his son on the ride home, "If you can't do any better than that, we might just as well stay home on Saturdays."

To him, the game wasn't for fun and it wasn't for exercise. The point of the whole activity was to win—end of subject.

Some young people look back on high school sports and thank their parents for the encouragement and discipline, but many more despise the pressure they felt from their parents.

A Lost Cause

Attempts to reduce sports pressure on teenagers seem futile. It comes from adults—parents and coaches—and shows no signs of waning. When winning is everything, mere participation is of little consequence, and that is a sad commentary on our times.

A father told me a story that is representative of many frustrated parents and crushed young people:

"I followed my kids from town to town. They weren't great basketball players, but they wanted to go out and they wanted to play. We traveled as far as ninety miles for some games because it was important to our teenagers that we be there. But game after game, even when there were big leads, the coach refused to put my boys in the game.

"You would think the coach would try to encourage the kids by putting them in the game. But the coach had a different agenda. Some team sport."

Someone needs to step back and assess the damage. Too many young people are crushed when a coach leaves them on the bench even when the game is no longer in doubt.

It's a tightrope walk for many parents—the attempt to show a reasonable amount of interest without drowning the young person with too much attention. They shouldn't be the center of attention, but they should be made to feel important, just like everyone else.

In Ephesians 6:4 fathers are warned not to exasperate their children. Don't frustrate them by creating unreasonable pressure. Parents must learn to be available to cheer them on without becoming the grave presence that makes each ball game a matter of life or death. Let's put sports in proper perspective, along with spelling bees, SAT tests, math exams, speech and debate contests, theater, science fairs, and memorization skills.

Fearful that their young people might fail, parents can raise their children's stress levels to equal that of an adult. Many teenagers encounter as much or more pressure than their parents. That might explain the high drug and alcohol abuse and the record suicide rate among that age group.

The Bible tells us not to be anxious about anything (Phil. 4:6). Yet we dump anxiety on our young people. Recently, a college student in Iowa shot several professors to death because he had been passed over for honors. What has happened to our value system? Anxiety will get to most of us if we don't lower the pressure level.

Measured Pace

Timing is all-important. Young people often need a gentle nudge, but not too hard, too early. As maturity and circumstances allow, they respond well to challenges.

It's the gift of the measured pace. We need to allow our teenagers to savor a variety of interests. Encourage them to search for themselves, to sample the competitive side, and yet take time for leisure, too.

One father noticed the unusual tension his daughter faced with her college studies, and suggested she drop out of school for a year. He gave her his permission to step back and cut the stress. She was young and had plenty of time. He suggested she spend the year enjoying life and discovering what was important to her. In this case, a father took the pressure off of excelling in school, and allowed his daughter to place the proper importance on becoming a whole, balanced human being.

In light of the many career changes most people make, what's the hurry? A young person may teach school for five years, sell insurance for six, and run a savings and loan operation for four. If they must be driven, let young people drive themselves. They shouldn't be driven by parents standing on the sidelines forcing them to excel at life.

Let's relax and enjoy life with our teenagers while we have them at home. Pressures will come soon enough. We don't have to be the number one country in mathematics. If we place third in the Olympics competition the earth will still rotate. And should Canada win the Stanley Cup we may wince and wheeze, but we will stagger on and survive.

Our young people will be grateful for all the attention we give them, but even more for a balanced view of living.

Donut
Runs and
Laughter

When is the last time your family sat around laughing uncontrollably? Not just a few muffled chuckles, but genuine side-aching, tears-in-your-eyes, down-to-your-toes laughing. Maybe it was at the dinner table on Thanksgiving afternoon, or huddled around a board game when something hit everyone as outrageously funny.

Laughing has a cleansing effect. It cuts the tension, makes the moment bright, develops a closeness in families. Humor rounds out life, puffing it up like a fresh pillow.

The best of family humor is never aimed to hurt anyone. It may involve a particular member, but it doesn't injure him. When a child drops the mashed potatoes in his lap he will probably get laughed at. If he is relaxed with his family, he will laugh, too. If he is uptight and feels singled out, the laughter by other family members can be painful. Teasing later on can be painful, too. However, an occasional blunder coupled with good-natured outbreaks of laughter is exactly what every family needs.

Playing games as a family can be a great experience if the game isn't taken too seriously. When teams are arranged and competitiveness isn't too severe, when no one's ego is on the line, when Dad doesn't have to have his way, and the males don't have to beat the females, games can provide fun, relaxing, and memorable family experiences.

But some young people remember family game time as terrorizing. It was an occasion when a big brother or an offensive uncle annihilated family members in a sport or game. Half the family was dragged into the activity, hating every moment of it.

Other families remember touch football in the park on autumn afternoons. Everyone got to play; everyone got a chance to be quarterback; everyone caught passes, and everyone dropped the ball. After the game, the family may have stopped off at the local drive-in for hot chocolate, and told exaggerated stories about what great heroes they had been.

Events like these jog the memory and warm the heart long after everyone has grown up and moved away. As young adults, these children remember how good it was whenever they see the leaves turning color, drive by a park, or see a football in a yard.

The children of summer games can still picture themselves on a baseball diamond or in an open field. The child stands at bat, Mom is stationed at first base, Dad is pitching, a sister is at third base and a brother in left field. As the ball is batted into the infield, everyone begins running in the same direction. In that child's memory, the yells and squeals of excitement still echo in the mind.

There are enough serious moments in life. There are the bleak times when a family member is sick or in trouble, or when finances are at an unusual low.

Those times need to be offset with times of fun, laughter, and games spent together as a family.

Too many young adults ache for those kinds of memories. Their minds are flooded with colorless sketches of a dreary childhood. Dad didn't wrestle with them on the floor; Mom didn't walk with them through the woods. It's up to parents to create good memories for their children.

Donut Runs

It's hard to know how to begin building memories, because children often pick up on traditions that parents never dreamed would be lasting.

Pat and I planned some events for the sole purpose of building a lasting memory, but many of those times have been completely forgotten. One example was the trip to the Truman Museum in Independence, Missouri. I ask you, what young person wouldn't be grateful for a three-hour tour of World War II paraphernalia?

I even took the girls to the Grand Old Opry in Nashville. I thought they'd be thrilled down to their sneakers to hear Hank, Skeeter, and Roy. Midway through the show I asked June how she was enjoying it. Her only reply was, "Do they have candy at the concession stand?"

And Mary said, "I'm glad you liked it, Dad," patting me on the shoulder like she had appeased me by going along.

Needless to say, those aren't memories our kids bring up frequently. (Evidently they weren't into culture.)

Instead, my girls remember the three of us stopping at a restaurant and buying a huge strawberry pie and eating the entire thing ourselves. They actually enjoyed pigging out more than visiting spectacular museums and hearing great country music.

They remember gorging themselves in a pizza parlor and then playing games like miniature bowling and shooting a phony basketball. Their idea of fun was talking to a mechanical bear and collecting prizes—toy harmonicas, chartreuse sunglasses, and a fuzzy key ring.

Another thing they remember fondly is a modern ritual: late night donut runs. Our ancestors didn't bring this tradition over from Copenhagen or Liechtenstein. This one was created in good old Nebraska.

Sometime around 11:00 P.M. someone in the house simply says, "Let's go for a donut run." Instantly, everyone dashes for the car for a go-as-you-are trip to Grand Island, twenty miles away. There we burst into the only all-night donut shop and scarf donuts for an hour or two. We may even talk about our diets. We laugh a little, dream a little, cry a little, and eat a lot. That usually continues until Pat zones off in a corner of the booth and someone suggests we take her home.

That's it! Granted, it isn't gathering around the yule log or making a pilgrimage to Memphis, but believe it or not that ritual has meaning.

When college studies cause tensions to rise, when bills get high, when relationships fall apart, our adult children long for a donut run. You may think they would head for a prayer tower, or a counselor, or sign up for the Peace Corps. Eventually they may do all of that. But high on the list are the therapeutic services rendered only by a donut run, or something similar.

Such an outing has all the ingredients necessary for wholeness. It breaks the routine, provides spontaneity, a change of scenery, an instant supply of ready listeners. It draws family members together, offers affordable food and drink, presents an open forum for opinions, and pumps enough sugar into the system to allow everyone to tiptoe to Pittsburgh.

Sometimes there is nothing like it. When life seems too complicated and the challenges too rough, an adult child will look back to the safe places he or she used to know. And they may not be the quiet moments and situations we tried to build into their memories. Rather, they often will be the odd nests and dens we accidently stumbled into. The possibilities are endless, but the opportunities must be supplied by us, the parents.

Other Traditions

Not every family is tied into a bakery of sorts. But most have some kind of "feel good" place. It might be a favorite cabin getaway. Maybe it's around the fireplace with a cup of hot cider. For some it's a coffee shop in the mall. Others come home to bake cookies because that's where they remember chats with Mom or siblings and warm food to soothe the soul. The smells and sounds of our favorite safe place give us a strong sense of healing and security.

Once young people have known a family gathering place like that, they are frequently drawn back to it. Eventually they meet a significant other who fills the role of going with them to fun places, but no one easily forgets walks with their parents, rides into the country, singing by the piano, a visit to the old church, crab cakes at the county fair, back rubs on the couch, or trimming the family Christmas tree.

These events bring warm, calming memories of childhood without making the young adult feel like a child. On the other hand, if a son comes home from college and his parents constantly tell him what to do, they reduce him to a child. If a daughter is only reminded of the mistakes she made in high school, her parents make her feel like a child again. But when parents provide the sounds and smells of the childhood environment, healing takes place.

A Good Place to Come Home To

For young people out on their own, going home to visit should bring more than serious talks and parental lectures. Out from under the parental umbrella of their childhood, they are looking for feelings of connection, security, identity, acceptance, comfort, and love. Some will admit to wanting to hear Dad pray before meals. They like to know the simple rituals of their childhood are still practiced. Not because they have a right or wrong quality, but because they give a feeling of security, warmth, goodness.

No one wants to go back to a place of turmoil. There is enough tension out in the world where they live every day. When they have a choice, young people will usually look for a place of peace and reassurance, of familiar, comfortable surroundings, an island where the spirit is uplifting and joyful. "A cheerful heart is good medicine, but a crushed spirit dries up the bones" (Prov. 17:22). If you wonder why your young people don't come home often, measure the level of cheerfulness in your home.

It's never too late to create a loving home, if there hasn't been one in the past. While several young children are living at home, there may be tension and turmoil, but when the family is grown, parents are often able to get back on an even keel and provide a tranquil haven for their children to return to. Ask yourselves what it would take to make your home more inviting. I'm not talking about a hot tub or outdoor pool. The secret is a home where young people feel accepted as they are, no questions asked.

A Place of Laughter

Home should be a place where the family lightens up. It doesn't have to be a comedy club, but neither should it be the war zone.

Laughter comes in different doses for different people. For one family, laughter may be spontaneous and constant. For another, it is occasional but warm. There is nothing right or wrong with either style. Young people who grew up in a family with a certain style of humor or fun-loving banter will usually appreciate that style when they return to visit.

To insure that teenagers remain comfortable with our style of humor, we need to keep in mind a couple of simple guidelines:

Don't allow humor that insults. It may get a laugh, but at the cost of wounding a family member's soul. Sooner or later someone will take personally what is meant in fun. If personal jokes and affronts are your style, begin to change. It may not be easy, but worth the effort if you want your teenagers to feel comfortable at home now, and return later where they feel safe.

When young people bring home friends or fiances, the newcomers will have trouble interpreting what's going on if the humor is harsh or fraught with innuendos. Many a prospective son-in-law or daughter-in-law is driven off by family humor they don't understand. It's hard to break into a family with this kind of humor.

Cut down on humor that recounts childhood stories. Some stories from childhood are funny, and bear repeating, but when told in front of friends or acquaintances they can also be painful. If you think a story's too good to pass up telling, think first how it may affect the young person you are telling about. Young adults don't like to come home to the uneasy feeling that their parents may embarrass them around others.

Simply stated, make laughter part of your family circle without hurting or embarrassing anyone. Like Brer Rabbit, we all need "a laughing place," but not one that inflicts pain. Let's laugh with each other, not at each other.

Being an Anchor— in a Time of Storm

A raging sea is an excellent metaphor to describe the teen years. Sometimes the waters are choppy, sometimes tumultuous. Seldom are they calm and placid. The sea may rest for a while, but it erupts again at the most unexpected times.

When the waves are tossing, every teenager needs to know they have an anchor in a dependable parent or parents.

Illness, broken hearts, crushed dreams, financial limitations, school problems, changes in the body, and spiritual turmoil are a few of the storms that rage in a teenager. Often teenagers appear to push their parents away in the midst of trouble. They need space, but in reality they don't want their parents to leave their side. They secretly expect them to hold steady no matter what.

The last thing teenagers need is a parent who does a disappearing act—here today, not around tomorrow, popping up on special occasions, showing up at the hospital or scene of an accident, and then forgetting birthdays or promised outings.

They also don't appreciate the parent who drifts out of the picture when storms darken the skies. When they are in trouble at school or on the streets, teenagers need parents who will drop anchor and ride out the rough seas right alongside them.

In this tentative, ever-changing society the temptation is to run from trouble. Some argue that they've done what they could to raise their children to be responsible adults, but can't waste their time on young people who cause difficulty or stray from the norm. Other parents stand by their teenagers, not defending wrongdoing, but continuing to show love and concern when problems surface. Fortunate is the young person who has parents who will not give up when the going gets rough.

The Difficult Years

Most parents have gone to the principal's office at least once because their child was in trouble at school. Some have stood at their side when they were accused of stealing; others have gone to special counseling with their child, or even visited a young member of their family in jail. We are talking about dependable parents. It's easy for a young person to feel grateful for parents like these.

Most teenagers seem to get into some kind of trouble during these turbulent years. There are so many opportunities to mess up, it's hard to avoid them all. Couple that with the fact that teenagers are testing the boundaries to see if they will budge. Like young birds trying out their wings, they are bound to stumble and fall in the process.

I can remember standing beside my children when they were in some kind of trouble. Sometimes they were completely innocent; other times they were as guilty as bank robbers. Either way, we stood by them, reminding them that we loved them no matter what.

One of the biggest surprises I faced when there was trouble involving my kids, was the tendency of parents to defend their teenager at the cost of attacking other parents or young people. It seems they needed to say that *their* teenager wasn't as bad as someone else's. I can understand the need to say something good about your own child, but not at the expense of putting someone else down.

Many parents become confused, disillusioned, and eventually bitter when their teenager's behavior is tearing them apart. It is hard for them to stand shoulder to shoulder with the child at times like that. Some parents will give up for short periods of time and then bounce back, others throw in the towel and quit trying.

The pressure can become unbearable. But the ultimate example for the Christian parent is God himself. He is never taken by surprise at our behavior, He doesn't cast us aside when we don't cooperate, and He never gives up on us. God practices extreme tolerance toward us, and that's the principle we need to put to work. The parent who doesn't give up on a wayward child provides an example of God's love that will remain in the memory of the teen.

The principle is both dependable and practical in a difficult parenting situation. We need to hang in there—maybe for a long time. Only the parent knows when a temporary "standing back" from the child

will be to the child's benefit, but the principle remains: Be an anchor even when their storm becomes
your storm.

The Fear of Abandonment

At every age a certain healthy fear is present. We
don't want to be left alone. Children, adolescents,
adults, and the elderly are no exception to this anxiety.

Your teenagers probably have friends who have
had one or both parents walk out on them. If not,
they have seen it portrayed on television, or read
about it in the newspaper. It is a common malady of
our day.

They've even heard about *good* parents who have
left their families. Parents who seem to have everything in order. Great communicators, good providers,
even Sunday school teachers and youth leaders.
Young people today have the nagging feeling that
abandonment could be a reality in any kind of family.
Even their own.

The teen years are self-centered years. Not because young people are intentionally selfish, but because changes come so rapidly in their young lives
that personal survival is a real issue in their minds.
They want to know how everything will affect them
personally and directly.

They expect their parents to stay around and take
responsibility like adults should. They don't want to
worry about dating, sex drive, sports, grades, awk-
wardness, zits, and keeping track of parents at the
same time. Something in life has to be dependable.
If they can't count on their hair staying in place, at
least they want their parents to stay in place.

An Imperfect World

Unfortunately, parents don't always come in neat packages. Frequently, divorce will disrupt a teenager's life. But any amount of stability is a welcome advantage. If both parents, regardless of their place of residence, do their best to support and encourage the young person, that teenager will benefit.

Few things are as devastating as the divorced parent who leaves the home and loses contact with his or her child. Some parents may imagine that their absence is best for the child, but that is far from true.

Just last week my wife and I asked each other if we had ever thought of leaving our family. The fact is, both of us had. I clearly remember standing in an airport in Minneapolis trying to decide which plane to catch. One plane would take me home to Nebraska, another to anywhere else.

Tired, depressed, and discouraged, I agonized over the decision. Not merely a fleeting thought, I tried to imagine where I could go and get lost. I even rationalized how much better off the children would be without me.

Somehow, by the grace of God, my legs moved sluggishly toward the gate marked home. I didn't hear the voices of angels or see bright lights that guided me toward my choice. It was rather a knowing, plodding kind of decision that led me back to the family I love.

I don't hesitate to tell that story because I have heard so many parents tell a similar one—like the parent who spent the weekend in a motel trying to decide which way to go; a father sitting in his car by the railroad tracks waiting for a train to pass and wondering whether to pull out in front of it.

Countless numbers have wrestled with a like decision. Those who pulled themselves up by their boot straps and went home, no doubt blessed their children beyond their imagination.

Someday our own children may face the same choice when they become parents. Perhaps at that moment they will draw strength from the realization that their own parents met the same crisis head-on and decided to go home.

In an imperfect world, young people don't need the added grief of being abandoned by a parent.

Family Conferences

Some teenagers become restless and impatient when their family gathers for serious talk or discussion. They may shift in their chairs, or hunch down as if to exclude themselves from the circle.

Despite the discomfort it may cause, family conferences are important and necessary. It is a time to collect information and to share true feelings. *What is going on and why?* Communication cannot be reduced to short sentences while passing in the hall or on the way out the door. Every family member has the right to know what is going on with other family members. And teenagers in the midst of change and difficulty especially need to know the anchor is in place, and someone is around to hear them out.

The Bible tells us that hope serves as an anchor. The seas cannot drive us away, neither will we drift apart in the night. "We have this hope as an anchor for the soul, firm and secure" (Heb. 6:19).

Our hope is founded in the unchangeable character of God. We know that when we wake up tomorrow morning God will not have turned fickle in the night. He will never be standing in an airport trying to decide which plane to catch. He will never leave us. Hope is an anchor because our loving Heavenly Father stands behind it.

But with human beings we can't be so sure. That's why a family needs to sit down together and discuss how things are going:

Do we still care about each other?
Are our finances still afloat?
Can we afford to take a trip?
How are Aunt Lydia's gallstones?
Why am I grounded?
Sara keeps taking my blouses without asking.
Are we moving or staying?
Do I have to go to church?

Some of these are critical issues, at a time when a teenager's busy life doesn't allow much contact with the rest of the family.

I was gone on a trip for a week. On the third day our son Jim asked quietly, "Is Dad gone someplace?" Surely we could have communicated better than that. Am I so dull that Jim didn't miss me for three days? Did I communicate so poorly that he didn't know I would be away? Communication needs to be a daily, conscious effort.

A Double Question

Take a security inventory of your home by asking yourself these questions:
1. What reasons does your teenager have for believing that you will still be around next week?
2. What reasons might your teenager have for believing that you may not be around next week?
After you sift through those two, then ask how you can shift more reasons away from question two and beef up the answers to question number one. Don't take either question lightly. Your teenager may perceive it quite differently than you do. Try to think of what things you say or do that could create sepa-

ration anxiety in a young, dependent person.

Careless comments about being unhappy at home or "around the children" can create anxiety in a young person. When we make derogatory remarks about our spouse—their other parent—the child may begin to wonder how stable their parents' relationship is. Strong references to being alone, or free, or separated in any way can give a child real cause for worry.

Reassuring phrases about love and hope, enjoying the childrens' company, pleasure over their presence, all help to reduce anxiety in a child. Much like we trust in God's character, young people depend upon the character of their parents. They need to know that we value commitment, relationships, family, and togetherness.

Every Octopus Needs a Head

Picture an octopus deep in the sea—its eight arms flailing in every direction. They can look very disjointed and uncoordinated. The only thing holding those tentacles together is the head. Without it, the creature is a jumble of arms.

When a family begins to pull apart, it needs a focal point to hold it together. One teenager in your household may break up with a boyfriend while another can't get a date. One may go out for a significant part in the school play and end up with a stand-in part. Another missed the honor society because of a home economics grade. You may have a teenager who is smoking pot, which makes the fight his brother got into at basketball practice seem minimal in comparison. Sibling rivalry is common. A sister thinks her older brother is a creep and her younger brother a nuisance.

Real and imagined troubles pull the family in different directions. Varying degrees of counsel and comfort are constantly needed. Parents must serve as the strong, central point of contact and order—even when they feel incapable.

Some parents may lose interest in keeping the family on an even keel, or even together. Some do walk away and let the children fend for themselves. But we are not really given that option. To abandon our family is to betray our own flesh and blood. All parents must master the feat of dealing with their own problems while solving those of their dependent children at the same time. No one seeing their family through crisis situations of varying proportions is free to stop parenting midstream. We are not really free to "find ourselves" or comb some undiscovered beach. God has placed children in our care to provide for them and be there for them as God is there for us.

And providing doesn't simply mean an allowance each week and three meals on the table. Emotional and spiritual stability are indispensable on the rocky sea of life.

A young man told of his periodic bouts with mental illness as a teenager. For a while he was institutionalized. But no matter how difficult his situation became, he said he could always count on his "indefatigable" dad. On visitors day at the state institution he would always see his father's smiling face. Even when the young man did bizarre things and made outrageous accusations, his father refused to give up.

A stable and responsible adult today, this young man owes his recovery in part to his father's steadfastness, and he is tremendously thankful for it.

The people that are usually put on pedestals as heroes are the swashbuckling types—rock stars, athletes, stars of stage and screen, adventurers. They all sound very romantic and wonderful, but the real heroes are the mothers and fathers who serve as anchors for their children. When everything else in a teenager's life turns to shifting sand, parents must be completely dependable and available. Your teens may not think of you as a hero today, but someday they will.

Bear Hugs
and Back
Rubs

Was Alice Frazier right or wrong? When Queen
Elizabeth II visited her in Washington, D.C., the sixty-
seven-year-old woman gave the Queen a hug. That
simple display of greeting and acceptance sent pro-
tocol watchers flapping. Is it ever proper for anyone
to squeeze the Queen without her initiating it?

While royal authorities try to unravel that dilemma, we turn our attention to more mundane issues. How important is it to establish a pattern of
family hugs and gentle touches? And can we main-
tain that practice during the teen years when personalities tend to bristle?

Anyone who has had a weary, stressed-out college student return home for a weekend realizes that
bear hugs and back rubs go a long way. Likewise any
young adult, whether working on a construction
crew or in an office, appreciates the physical contact
of a loving parent.

Even when words fail, the soothing, accepting

message received through physical contact succeeds. Young people (unless they have been physically abused) usually hunger for the touch of a mother or father, sending the message that they are still loved and accepted.

Picture a young adult coming through the door and being embraced by a loving parent. Instant rapport is established. Imagine that same person relaxing in a chair while the parent rubs his or her neck and shoulders. That simple expression of gentle care sends a message of love deep into the bones as no words can.

Not only is the loving touch enjoyed by parent and child, but it is therapeutic for siblings. Brothers and sisters who battled as small children find a sense of closeness by entering each other's embrace, or placing a loving hand on a shoulder or arm.

It isn't easy for everyone to reach out and touch someone, but that doesn't mean it shouldn't be done. Some stoic parents have to hurdle generations of coolness in order to reach out to their children. Many parents have literally saved a relationship with their children because they suddenly grew arms and learned how to use them. They may have exhausted every other form of communication when a hug served as a lifesaver. It took great courage to toss that life preserver out, but they mustered the strength to do it.

Common Ages for Hugging

It's too simple to say we are huggers or we aren't huggers. Parents are often good huggers at the young stages and hold back when the children get older. Some parents are *bundle huggers.* They love to hold an infant. They rock the baby, utter nonsensical phrases, and sing lullabies. The first year or so they can't keep their hands off the little bundle.

By the time the child is two, the cuddly baby has turned into a wind-up toy wound a few notches too tight. The toddler is into house demolition and a bit less apt to snuggle in to your arms. Many parents leave the hugging stage at this point—never to return.

One of our children became a bucking horse at that stage. Any attempt to hold or rock the child was greeted with flailing arms, kicking feet, and a head smashing into your unprotected nose. One minute of struggling and battering convinced you to put the child down and let him spin for himself.

Other parents like to hold grade-school children. They could be called *simplicity huggers.* Grade-school children tend to be innocent and unsophisticated. It's like holding fresh air. They are anxious to learn and eager to please. Most of them believe their parents are heroes.

It's easy to hug young children when they've been gone all day and return home from school. You sit close on the couch and go over homework with them, or talk about what they did at school. Some parents who weren't so great at the bundle stage become great simplicity huggers.

Toward the end of grade school the child stretches out to become an adolescent or teenager. Hugging now drops in popularity faster than the stock market in October. Parents who can hug during the teen years are *hero huggers.* They hold on when it is most difficult and yet most needed. There is a special place in the parents' hall of fame for teen huggers.

Embracing a teenager is like hugging a track star in motion. How do you put your arms around a person who is running away from you? Most young people are trying to find their identity, and distance themselves from their parents. Hugging these kids is a Herculean feat.

Despite its difficulty, hero hugging is well worth the effort. It is an emotional bridge between adolescence and adulthood. Teenagers need the contact during the turmoil years and into the years when they will revert back to appreciating their parents.

As we mentioned in an earlier chapter, while teenagers push away from their parents, they are desperately hoping their parents will not really leave them alone. Many parents back off entirely during this time. It's understandable, because they feel repulsed. But it's a test. Teenagers want to know if you will reject them while they are rejecting themselves. They want to be assured that their parents will accept them no matter how they behave.

Innovative Hugging

Sometimes you have to be creative. If your teen doesn't want to be out-and-out hugged, you may have to come at it in another way.

As a teenager, Jim didn't like it when I hugged him, but he loved to wrestle with me on the floor. Like many fathers and sons, we pushed back the furniture and went at it. Jim, at sixteen, tried out his newly learned wrestling holds on me.

I wish Jim had enjoyed a conventional hug now and then, but his idea of a hug was always to get me in a hold on the floor. The important thing is that it allowed us to touch each other. If it was his way of reaching out to me, I was all for it. Now that Jim is older, we simply tug at each other in the foyer when he arrives home and occasionally hold hands while we pray at the table. (I don't know how much longer I could have kept up our rough-and-tumble relationship anyway.)

Putting an arm around the shoulders of a young person has a positive effect, believe me. To take their hand in ours while talking to them is like connecting emotional lines. The nerve endings send messages to the brain and to the soul. Flesh *does* need the touch of other flesh, and not just in a sexual context.

We actually suffer when we are deprived of human touch. And many young people get into moral trouble when they are starved of physical contact at home.

Hugging the Rebels

Rebellious teenagers are no doubt the most difficult to hug. Like rambunctious two-year-olds, they lash out at everything. They are in pain, and it's easy for them to cause pain to others, even unknowingly.

But we must find a way. If at all possible, slide in among the flying shrapnel and put your hands on him or her in a loving way. They need the calming effect of the touch of a loving parent.

Often prodigals believe they are not worth hugging. They raise their prickly quills and try to ward off anyone who comes too close. It takes a genuine hero to move in and put an arm around them. We may get hurt by trying, but we must at least try. Parents do well to let the rebelling teen know that he or she isn't as unlovable as they may imagine.

Sometimes touch is the only way to communicate how much we care. Words fail, or will not be heard.

Reluctant Huggers

Many parents who fared well as *bundle huggers,* and later as *simplicity huggers,* fall apart at the thought of becoming *hero huggers.* Often they have deep-seated fears about the sexual connotations of hugging a blossoming girl or boy. These insecurities hold them back from fully embracing someone they love.

If the fear of hugging because of sexual connotation is a result of your own childhood experience of sexual abuse, you must seek counsel for yourself so as not to deprive your child of valuable physical contact.

If reluctance to embrace a child comes from a lack of embracing in your own childhood, or a personality that simply doesn't "hug," you need to break the ice. It is all right to touch someone. If you don't believe it, talk about it with your spouse. Get assurance from someone close to you that it is all right to embrace your teenager.

My wife is a prime example of someone who is not by nature a hugger. Physically reserved, Pat has never been one to embrace everyone who comes through the door. But by some miracle, she is a mother who broke the ice, and could wrap her arms around her teenagers without hesitation, and hug until their eyes bulged.

Even during the days when our teenagers were hardheaded and defiant, Pat worked all the harder at embracing the gremlins. In fact, she seemed to sense that they needed hugs the most when they were the least approachable.

The Healing Touch

When June tumbled down the stairs at home, she dislocated her shoulder. She spent the afternoon in the local hospital in considerable pain. When the shoulder was in place again and she had rested, we took her home.

Later I asked June what the experience was like. She said there was a great deal of pain, but "While Dr. Larson talked to me," she explained, "telling me what they would have to do to reset the shoulder, he put his hands on my good arm. Just having him hold my good arm did more to calm me down than anything else."

The power of touch is an enormous healing resource. Not just physical healing, but mental, emotional, and even spiritual.

In the New Testament, we are told that early Christians touched and kissed often. Not only did they practice physical contact, but their writings encourage every believer to do it.

They embraced (Acts 20:36–38). They kissed (Rom. 16:16). Jesus washed their feet (John 13:5). They laid hands on people when they prayed (Acts 6:6). Jesus touched people when He healed them (Matt. 8:3).

Bear hugs and back rubs are more than a modern psychological discovery. Like chocolate, touching has long had a soothing, sedating effect on people.

At times of grief, whatever we say or don't say to the grieving person, our touch is certain to be comforting. The simple act of holding the person's hand helps to bring reassurance and understanding.

And loving touch can peel a distraught teenager off the walls. Words and accusations will often drive them to distraction, while a gentle touch has been known to reduce anxiety and increase trust.

A soldier reported that after serving in Viet Nam, he hired a prostitute the first night he arrived in California. He paid her to simply hold him. He needed a hug badly, and was willing to pay for it.

There are no guarantees that we can heal everyone by merely touching them. We can't bring solace to every soul or mend every relationship with a hug. Likely it will take much more than that to transform a wayward teenager. But it's a start. It bridges a gap; it meets a felt need in every human being. It could help your teens today, and it could bring them back tomorrow.

Seeing Parents Touch

Parents who hold and hug each other in front of their children wrap a warm security blanket around the entire family. In past generations parents were reluctant to make any physical contact when the children were around, but today most realize that touching sends an extremely important message. Children, young and older, need to know and see for themselves that their parents are getting along. To see them close, even playful, expressing their affection for one another should not be an embarrassment to anyone. Rather, it assures children that all is well between the two most important people in their lives.

When teenagers go on to establish their own families, they will be thankful for the model of expressed affection that they had at home. They may have less trouble with intimacy in their own marriage because they were accustomed to seeing their parents close. Those young people who have no example to follow often find the adjustment of being close to someone difficult. We actually owe it to our children to allow them to see us expressing our love with hugs, kisses, and gentle caresses. Otherwise, they will likely feel uncomfortable displaying affection in front of their children.

A New Way of Touching to Some

A simple display of gentle touching may not be familiar to some families. In some backgrounds touching meant aggression, or had sexual connotations. Some parents push their children or strike them to affirm their authority. They may understand a gentle touch only with regard to sexual overtones.

These two misconceptions are unfortunate, because children are deprived of the feeling of parental security that is conveyed through a loving touch or embrace.

Too many fathers are ambivalent over the issue of touching. They have a hard time imagining holding a female close to them without being aroused sexually. Fathers must gain control over this fear, and seek help if necessary. Teenage daughters especially need the warmth and security of an embrace from their father. It bridges the gap for them from adolescence to womanhood and lessens their need for excessive contact with boys their own age too soon.

With stepfathers the issue may be even more difficult. Because a stepdaughter is not a blood relative, the stepfather may have trouble handling any kind of intimacy. Though care should be taken in any expression of affection, it is not impossible to show love to children of all ages and relationships in a discreet manner.

Mothers are not exempt, of course. Some studies even indicate that a mother's touch is more of a confidence builder than a father's. But both parents can have a positive effect on their children by touching, from the time of infancy on through adolescence.

How comfortable a teenager is with touching depends to a large degree on how comfortable his parents are with it. If a parent's contact is tense, uneasy, awkward, the young person will tend to feel the same way. The parents may even convey by their actions that there is something wrong with touching, but they are going to do it anyway.

Separation Anxiety

As children grow into adolescence, they frequently try to avoid all physical contact with their parents. It is part of their effort to disconnect, to become independent, whether conscious or unconscious. This attempt to separate can have a serious downside. The lack of physical contact can result in heightened separation anxiety. A strange paradox. The more teens pull away from their parents, the more distanced they feel. And the more distanced, the greater the anxiety.

By pulling back, teenagers receive what they want: distance. But the very distance creates results in feelings of isolation and despair.

Later, as teenagers mature, they again sense a strong need to get close to their parents. That's when parental persistence pays off. If parents continue to reach out and touch their children even when they shrink from it, the children are better able as mature teenagers to re-enter that realm of intimacy they knew with their parents.

Even animals have a need for touching and affection. That's why your cat or dog rubs against your leg occasionally. You automatically respond to the animal because you recognize its need. Teenagers need to be touched. The problem is that they have conflicting needs of intimacy and distance. They may send mixed signals, because they live with dual urges to flee and draw close at the same time.

Parents need to reach across the teen's conflict and make contact by some means or another. When you do, you create a sense of intimacy between yourselves and your children that will serve them in good stead now and in the future.

Ground-
ing Me

If you could eavesdrop on a group of middle-aged adults talking about their parents, you would probably notice the tone turning melancholic when the discussion reaches the subject of discipline. They may speak wistfully of their parents' attempts to set boundaries, with comments like:

> I could not break the curfew or my dad would ground me.
>
> I stayed out until 2:00 A.M. and lost the car for two weeks.
>
> All my dad did was give me *that look*, and it made me feel terrible.
>
> If I didn't keep my grades up my parents would kill me (a phrase often used to describe parents who actually did their children no physical harm, but made it very clear what was expected of them).

There is a certain nostalgia about good discipline. There is even a longing by some who wish they had received more discipline. They wish their parents had set firmer limits and enforced them more frequently.

It is true that teenagers crave healthy discipline. Sometimes they find it difficult to control themselves and they would *like* someone else to help them with that control. They will protest the discipline at the time, but in most cases look back at discipline with great appreciation.

June used to confuse us by asking for discipline. Before going to a party she would ask, "What if I don't get home on time? You're going to ground me, aren't you?" Or, "You're going to make me work in the yard, aren't you?" Or, "You're going to take the television away, aren't you?"

And we would say, "Don't worry about it, June. Just be home on time." June was always home on time. I believe she was looking for two things. *One,* she wanted to know there was a controlling factor watching over her, and she wanted to know someone cared. *Two,* June wanted to tell her friends, "If I'm late getting home my dad is going to kill me."

Actually, the statement could be called an endearing acknowledgement. It's a gross exaggeration with a microscopic trace of truth. The young person who says this probably has a healthy respect for a parent who could apply reasonable pressure.

When They Won't Be Grateful

There are three types of discipline that cause resentment instead of thankfulness:

1. The absence of any boundaries
2. Unreasonable discipline
3. Cruel discipline

Adults who look back at discipline in their young lives as a *grim* memory, obviously are not appreciative of it. They see the act of discipline as something other than an act of love. In their case, their parents were cruel, self-serving, vindictive.

Discipline that is born out of a parent's selfishness, a need to assert authority, or a need to look strong or tough, is discipline that will be resented by the child. Young people can usually sense when parents don't really have the child's best interest at heart. They know when there is another motive at the root. That bewilders the teenager and eventually frustrates him. *Frustration turns to anger; anger turns to hate.*

Spanking a child should never be done out of anger. If you cannot control yourself when your child misbehaves, you'd better not spank him or her. Discipline and spanking are not synonymous. There are many ways to discipline without causing physical pain.

If you think you are spanking in rage, or your spouse feels that you are, you may be doing exactly that. Discipline that is extended out of anger will cause lasting anger and resentment in the child or young person that receives it, because they will sense that they are being abused.

When correction is needed, discipline of some kind is in order. A teenager out of bounds needs to be brought back within those bounds for his or her own good. It isn't an easy task and some forms of discipline simply do not work with teenagers. They are not little children who can be picked up and placed in a corner. Discipline for a teenager must be tempered and meted out with wisdom and discretion. If your teen defies discipline there may be little or nothing you can do immediately. But don't give up. When children sense you are in this for their own good, they will eventually respond and be grateful for your efforts.

A Biblical Perspective

Hebrews 12:7–11 gives us an overview of the benefits of sound discipline. While referring to the discipline of our Heavenly Father, it reminds us of the principles of parental discipline:

1. *Good parents discipline* (v. 7).

Parental discipline is a sign that a child is accepted by the parent. If we refuse to discipline, we have in a sense rejected the child.

2. *Children respect discipline* (v. 9).

If discipline is carried out correctly and lovingly, young people will usually respect their parents for drawing boundaries and enforcing them.

3. *Discipline is not pleasant at the time* (v. 11).

Don't expect your teenager to congratulate you when you discipline him or her. The process is painful. No one likes being corrected or criticized.

4. *Later, it produces righteousness and peace* (v. 11).

As they grow older, young people see and reap the benefits of a disciplined home life. They can look back and see their parents' efforts as a labor of love. They are thankful that their mother or father gave them guidelines, boundaries, and deadlines, even if they seemed painful at the time.

If God disciplines those children whom He loves and calls sons, we as good parents should also discipline our children and thereby show them our love and concern for their lives.

Discipline As a Form of Communication

The tendency of parents who don't talk to their teenagers is to use discipline as a major form of communication.

From early childhood, children test their parents' patience and communication skills. Who hasn't seen a mother try to calmly communicate some instruction to a preschool child, only to become frustrated at the lack of response from her little one? If the mother is tired or busy she may resort to using her hand or the nearest object to get the child's immediate attention.

Obviously, striking a child is not a good way to communicate your wishes. Too many parents use discipline as a first or major form of communication, thereby defeating the real purpose of discipline, which is to correct defiance, disobedience, or unacceptable behavior. Words fail, or habit makes it easier to resort to some degree of force.

Parents do well to practice verbal skills, to make a concentrated effort to communicate boundaries, rules, necessary limits. If a rule later seems too rigid, don't be afraid to be flexible. Fairness and understanding go a long way in promoting good responses in your children. Don't discipline your child without the child knowing the reason for the discipline. Children need guidelines and they will generally abide by them if they see love and consistency being demonstrated on their behalf.

Good Discipline; Bad Results

Practical parents understand that discipline has limited results. Even if a parent has perfected good discipline in the home, there is no guarantee the results will be lasting.

That's why the book of Proverbs admonishes young people to heed good discipline. Teenagers may choose to bolt and go their own way no matter how well their parents practiced good discipline. It doesn't mean the parent was wrong or right, it just means the teen made his or her own choice to go against their upbringing. Most will return to the way they were taught, but again there are no guarantees.

Some teenagers flatly refuse to accept any form of guidance. Even when they know the discipline is for their own good, they may still reject it. They are determined to make their own way and live with the consequences.

As a result, many parents are too hard on themselves. They wonder what they did wrong, where they failed, when their children are trapped in alcohol, drugs, premarital sex, crime, or a religious cult. The temptation of the parents is to blame themselves.

Some parents have failed their children. They were not consistent in discipline, they dealt it in anger, or they did not discipline at all. But many others did the best they could. These parents should not flog themselves for teens they couldn't control.

Disappointed Parents

It's hard to look at old photos of children who have rebelled and rejected your discipline. You may see yourself camping with a son who grew up to chase a wild life. Or you look at your wayward daughter in her younger days when she was so sweet and adored her daddy. You fight back tears trying to comprehend how she could have turned away and become so unhappy.

It hurts to look at pictures of the whole family in happier times, and single out a child whose whereabouts you are uncertain of today. Photos offer pleasant memories, but they also remind us of broken dreams, disappointments, and uncertain destinies.

When teenagers become raging rivers determined to jump their banks, there isn't much that even the most dedicated parent can do.

Correct discipline is not an easy task. It takes the grace of God and lots of hard work, but when those days are over many young people look back with gratitude and love to parents who gave it their best shot.

Not Pitting
Us Against
Each Other

When Jim brought home a school paper with a grade of ninety-eight percent, we stood on chairs and cheered. We made every effort to let him know what a good job he had done and how proud we were of him. God gave Jim a first-class mind, and we made him aware of it.

But later the same day, Jim found out how his sisters fared in their schoolwork. Jim's outstanding ninety-eight score came in third behind his two sisters. This, of course, took some of the shine from Jim's feeling of accomplishment. It turned to a sour I-can't-win-no-matter-what feeling.

Competition among siblings can be a lifelong problem. Someone is going to get the bigger house, the higher degree, the higher wage, the richer spouse, the fancier car, maybe even better health. If our children grow up to measure their worth by how they compare to their siblings they are pitted against each other for a lifetime.

Parents may not be able to control all sibling rivalry but they can be sensitive to it. They especially need to resist the temptation to pick favorites. Young people already imagine that their parents like one child more than the other. Unfortunately, sometimes it's a fact. Check your attitudes and try to show equal love and concern for all your children.

Love the Disobedient One

God loves us even when we're bad. His love is consistent and unfailing, not dependent on our behavior.

As parents, we tend to love good behavior more than bad behavior. If we have a rebellious or defiant teenager, we tend to love him or her less.

We would be less than honest if we said that our feelings for a troublesome child never hit bottom. We feel rejected ourselves when our love or discipline or lifestyle are rejected. Don't knock yourself for occasionally feeling angry about the behavior of your teenager. The feeling is normal. But don't take the anger out on your child. Hate the behavior; love the child.

Anyone can love an obedient child. The test of love is when you express it to a disobedient child. Of course you want your kid to get straight A's, keep a neat room, and volunteer to do the dishes. But when he sneaks out, lies to you, and makes his sister's life miserable, love him anyway.

Recently a mother said, "Frankly, a lot of times I don't like my son. He seems to work hard at wrecking my life."

Exactly. He is extremely difficult to love at that point. Admit it. Having said that, then look to Christ for the help it will take to love him anyway. To love a teenager when he or she is unlovely is the challenge of a Christian parent. *And it's tough.*

When we hear testimonies of converted prisoners who are able to love an abusive guard, we want to applaud and shout. Wouldn't it be fantastic if we were strong enough to be that kind of Christian? In our case the challenge may be to love an abusive teenager who is effectively wrecking our family. The Holy Spirit can give us that kind of love.

We are encouraged by the fact that while we were still sinners, Christ died for us (Rom. 5:8). And though we were disobedient, we have received mercy (Rom. 11:30).

Our Children Are Like Us

God must see us as the rebellious teenager from time to time. We insist on our own way; we refuse to follow orders; we are uncooperative and defiant. Kicking and screaming, we refuse to buckle under and do what we know God is asking us to do.

Maybe we don't like to see the comparison. But in many cases it is a valid one. It may help us to remember that God wrestles over the same disobedience in us as we do in our children.

No Two Will Be Alike—Love Them Equally

Love the doctor; love the dancer; love the adventurer.

The first step is to ask ourselves on what basis do we love our teenager:

on the basis of performance?
on the basis of behavior?
on the basis of career choice?
on the basis of potential?
on the basis of compliance?
on the basis of need?

because they belong to us?

If we love them solely because they are ours, we are less likely to allow other factors to affect that love.

Smart parents don't compare. Each child is a unique personality. Each has different qualities, capabilities, and interests.

Parents may ask, "Why can't you get good grades like your sister?" or "Why can't you behave like your brother?" or "Why can't you keep your room clean like the other kids do?" Teenagers look for evidence that suggests their parents prefer another sibling over them. In the totem pole of life, teenagers want to know where they fit in. They will grab hold of any hint that suggests they are on the bottom of the pole.

Often parents have to work hard at keeping the balance in their minds. Their math has to go something like this:

A cheerleader is equal to a bookworm.
An athlete is equal to an artist.
A homebody is equal to a class president.
A chess player is equal to a pole vaulter.
A singer is equal to a good speller.

And so it goes. No child should be treated more favorably than another because of his or her choice of activity or talent. Each needs the reassurance that he or she is equal to every other member of the family.

One child may need a tutor. It's not likely all your children will need one, but meet the legitimate need of the one who does. When one child goes through a tough stage, take the child out for a special snack or outing as often as necessary. Don't hold back because you can't afford to take every child out every time. Meeting individual needs is not showing favoritism.

Children can easily understand attention shown to one child when he or she needs it, when they know they will get the help they need when they need it.

For instance, I took my son camping alone but never took either daughter alone. Camping was something the girls didn't want to do or need to do at the time. It would have been foolish of me to say that I couldn't take Jim because it wouldn't be fair to the girls. I found other things to do with them.

We took one daughter to pick out furniture and set up her dorm room. Our other daughter chose to go off on her own, decorated her own place, and then invited us to come see it.

I know a father who refused to take one child out alone when he couldn't take all four. He claimed he was treating them equally. To me, that is not equality. Our love and concern for each child should be equal, but attention at certain times is different according to needs and circumstances. What one child desperately needs, the other child might be repulsed to receive. It makes as much sense as bandaging the fingers of all the children because one child has a cut.

Make each child feel special in his or her own right, and he or she will feel equal to the other children in the family.

Jacob's Big Blunder

Every parent should read Genesis 37 often. Jacob, the aging father of thirteen sons, chooses Joseph to be his favorite. He should get the knucklehead award. Joseph was seventeen years old and next to the youngest, but Jacob made it obvious he was his number-one son.

No subtle move, Jacob had a special coat of many colors designed especially for Joseph, demonstrating to his twelve brothers that he was the favorite. To top it off, Jacob appointed this teenager to report on his brothers when they were away from home.

Joseph soon began bragging to the others about his dreams. In each, he was clearly superior to his brothers. Before long even Joseph's doting father became fed up with this behavior.

Of course when his brothers saw their father's obvious favoritism, they hated Joseph. Soon they devised ways to either abandon Joseph, kill him, or hand him over to slave traders.

No one suggests that the behavior of the brothers was correct. Nor would we agree that Joseph's needling of his brothers with the substance of his dreams was acceptable. But Jacob's behavior was also unacceptable. To pit sibling against sibling is to pack a stick of dynamite and light the fuse.

During a radio talk-show a woman called in to describe to me how her mother had tried to pit her children against each other. She would tell one child a story about another in order to get the one riled up against the other. The caller said she saw it as an attempt by her mother to keep the children running to her to find more pieces to the continuously shifting puzzle—a bizarre way of drawing the children to herself and away from siblings.

The host of the show interrupted to protest that mothers don't do things like that. Unfortunately, some do exactly that.

Coming Home

As I write this chapter, I see by the calendar that next week is Thanksgiving. All our grown children plan to be home for the celebration. All of us get along well, even though there were some extremely rough times when they were younger.

Hopefully as each of them drives down Interstate 80 they will have good thoughts about home and about how we as their parents feel about them. We both made a conscious effort to make each feel loved, accepted, and wanted. I like to think we were successful.

We cared about their victories and their losses, their strengths and their failures as individuals. We may not have felt exactly the same love for each one every day. We are too human for that kind of perfection. Some days we were bewildered by their attitudes and behavior. But by the grace of God we kept love at the forefront, and I think we conveyed fairness and acceptance for each one of them for who they are.

As we gather around the Thanksgiving table at our house, I know that no one will bring up an insulting remark made in the past, or mention a failed promise of yesterday. I don't think any of us has ugly baggage to carry over. We dealt with issues as they came up. No one will demand an explanation for behavior present or past. God has enabled us to love each other in spite of differences, in spite of disagreements. I am extremely grateful for this. Not everyone looks forward to a peaceful special occasion with their grown children.

Pitted Against Parents

While on the subject of pitting children against children, or showing favoritism, mention should be made of parents who lord it over their grown children, making them feel less than adult.

Recently a young woman confided in me how much she hates going home for the holidays. She said all her grown brothers and sisters and their families gather for special occasions and their seventy-year-old father reigns supreme.

After the meal has been completed and the table has been cleared, the father will break out the same old games. That would be all right, she explained. Old games could bring back good memories. But her father not only insists on playing the games, he also insists on winning them.

The old gent will badger and browbeat and make everyone play again and again until he has won. Only then will he sit back, content that he is still the champion of the family.

No wonder the children hate to go home. They feel two unbearable pressures. First, they must play the games Dad wants or he becomes cranky. Second, they must play until Dad wins or he becomes wounded and pouts. Not a pleasant picture, but one that is probably repeated in other homes over the holiday season.

While parents must avoid pitting young people against each other, neither should they "challenge" their own children, asserting their own authority and position each time the clan comes home. It will become a burden that most young adults will want to escape.

Equal Value

What is valuable to us in our children? Grades? Appearance? Compassion? Obedience?

For the ideal answer we must turn to Jesus Christ. The Son of God died for just one value: personhood. He didn't give himself for the swift or the lovable or the bright or the cooperative. While we were disobedient, Christ died for us.

If we can love our children simply because of who they are, regardless of what they do or how they do it, it is possible to love them all equally. If we insist on using another scale (i.e., judging them by their grades, appearance, cooperation, etc.) it will be impossible to love them equally.

Our children will never be identical. One will always be something more or less than the other. We must love each of them for who they are. Love based on performance will fail.

Equal Acceptance

The system by which many people love their children is easy to test. Spend thirty minutes talking to a young adult who feels rejected because of less-than-desirable performance. That person can never measure up to his parents' expectations.

"My parents are disappointed in me," Brendon explained sadly. "I'm not what they had in mind. I didn't go to college; I married early, and I don't ever expect to be a deacon at the Baptist Church. When I go home I can still see the pain in their faces. It's like their 'big failure' has come home and they feel so sorry for me.

"I could live with myself if only they could get that pain off their faces."

Brendon has felt rejected all his young life, the one who seemed to mess up everything he touched. He flunked on performance. He failed his parents' expectations. Hopefully someday they will discover the importance of loving a child for *who he is* not *what he does.*

When a parent is a believer in acceptance according to performance, that value-system rubs off on their children. Brendon has trouble accepting himself because his parents have devalued him.

Equal acceptance of each of our children is a large order. Many parents struggle with it. Those who succeed in loving their children equally are those who center on people-love, not performance-love. Thank God for parents who see the difference.

Some Final Thoughts

Common sense tells us not to go hunting with a blindfolded sharpshooter. Regardless of his skills, he will need to see the target clearly. Otherwise, he will be shooting at snapping twigs and rustling leaves.

When God gives children to couples they are usually very excited about the possibilities. They look forward to years of love, growth, fun times, challenges, and feelings of fulfillment, accomplishment. Most are grateful to God for the opportunity to share what they know and have experienced with the young lives entrusted to them.

The whole process is more satisfying if the blindfolds are removed and the targets seen clearly. That way, time isn't wasted circling around, aiming at nothing in particular. Parenting at its best has an idea of what it wants to accomplish. By establishing goals, we are less likely to frustrate everyone by giving conflicting messages.

I'm not going to give you a list of goals. Those are for you as parents to decide. Probably the most important thing to remember is to remain flexible. Goals may change to meet the individuality of your family. And keep a sense of humor at all costs.

Parenting does have tremendous rewards. For innumerable parents, children give meaning and enrichment to their lives. But parenting also has some headaches and heartaches. There is probably no family who hasn't had some painful disappointments.

But no one would trade in their children to escape pain or disappointment. That would be like giving up your hopes, your dreams, your faith. Children are energetic, unpredictable, and a lot of hard work, but they also bring lots of joy, happiness, and spontaneity into our lives. Who would want to protect their hearts from pain and give up the flipside of parenting?

Effective parenting knows both its limitations and its potential. Even great parenting cannot guarantee the outcome of a child's life, cannot always control a teenager's behavior, cannot force moral attitudes, cannot perceive the final product. We need to remind ourselves of that. But good parenting can aim for the right values, show consistent love, teach self-control, model forgiveness, demonstrate faith in Jesus Christ, display courage, and infuse hope and optimism. Effective parenting makes the tools available to the young person so that he or she can choose a complete life.

But even though we may make every tool available, the child may choose not to use those tools. All children are equipped with their own free will. We strengthen their wings, teach them how to fly, and then let them go. That's the hard part.

Thank God for parents who aim for the right goals and give their children unconditional love. These kids have a chance at wholeness and a sense of belonging.

Parenting is close to the heart of God. After all, God is the Greatest Parent.

Books by William Coleman
from Bethany House Publishers

CHESAPEAKE CHARLIE SERIES
Chesapeake Charlie and the Bay Bank Robbers
Chesapeake Charlie and Blackbeard's Treasure
Chesapeake Charlie and the Haunted Ship
Chesapeake Charlie and the Stolen Diamond

DEVOTIONALS FOR FAMILIES WITH YOUNG CHILDREN
Animals That Show and Tell
Before You Tuck Me In
Getting Ready for Our New Baby
If Animals Could Talk
Listen to the Animals
My Hospital Book
My Magnificent Machine
Singing Penguins and Puffed-Up Toads
Today I Feel Like a Warm Fuzzy
Today I Feel Shy
Warm Hug Book

DEVOTIONALS FOR TEENS
Earning Your Wings
Friends Forever

It's Been a Good Year
Knit Together
Measured Pace
Newlywed Book
Ten Things Your Teens Will Thank You For . . . Someday
Today's Handbook of Bible Times and Customs
What Children Need to Know When Parents Get Divorced